*Man, Woman, and
the Meaning of Love*

Dietrich von Hildebrand

Man, Woman, and the Meaning of Love

God's Plan for Love, Marriage, Intimacy, and the Family

SOPHIA INSTITUTE PRESS®
Manchester, New Hampshire

Man, Woman, and the Meaning of Love was first published as *Man and Woman* in 1966 by Franciscan Herald Press. Henry Regnery Company issued a paperback edition in 1967. In 1992, Sophia Institute Press published an edition that preserved the essential content of those earlier editions (most of it word-for-word), but contained dozens of new subheadings and a completely new order of topics. This 2002 edition, a retitled reprint of the 1992 edition, is published by Sophia Institute Press with permission of Alice von Hildebrand.

Sophia Institute Press®
Box 5284, Manchester, NH 03108
1-800-888-9344
www.sophiainstitute.com

Nihil obstat: Marion A. Habig, O.F.M.
Imprimatur: Most Rev. Cletus F. O'Donnell, D.D.
December 9, 1965

Library of Congress Cataloging-in-Publication Data

The Library of Congress has catalogued an earlier
edition of this work as follows:

Von Hildebrand, Dietrich, 1889-1977
    Man and woman: love and the meaning of intimacy / Dietrich von
    Hildebrand.
        p. cm.
    ISBN 0-918477-14-X; 1-928832-44-X (pbk. : alk. paper)
        1. Man-woman relationships. 2. Love — Religious aspects — Christianity.
        3. Marriage. 4. Friendship. I. Title.
HQ801.V66 1992
92-19822 305.3 — dc20   CIP

Contents

Introduction

⚘

Although we hear that sex is overemphasized today, this is not correct. Rather, we live in a time in which sexuality is no longer understood in its true nature. People today are generally as blind to its true meaning as are persons who completely lack sensuality.

A sterile approach to sexuality dominates our time. Out of boredom, people have granted to casual, shallow, and neutralized sex a distorted role.

Today's blatant sexuality conceals a pathetic sensual emptiness. For sex is a mystery. It is a pity that so much writing on the subject deals with sex exclusively from the moral point of view, rather than attempting to probe this mystery of sex. For it is only when one has grasped the nature, meaning, and value of sex that one is equipped to understand the moral values and disvalues in this sphere.

Many people praise the free and objective approach to sex in our days as compared with the Victorian age of prudery or with the puritanical horror of all things sexual. Certainly the prude and the Puritan are unfortunate, but not because they feel shame nor because they abstain from dealing with this sphere as if it were something neutral.

Man, Woman, and the Meaning of Love

No, what is wrong with the Puritan approach is its despising of sexuality. It sees sex as something base in itself, as morally negative, which precisely denies the high mission to which this sphere is destined — to serve the ultimate mutual donation in spousal love. This spousal love between man and woman is not a romantic invention of the poets but a tremendous factor in human life from the very beginning of the history of mankind: the source of the deepest happiness in human earthly life. Of it, the Song of Solomon says: "If a man shall give all the substance of his house for love he shall despise it as nothing."[1] Indeed it is this love alone which is the key to an understanding of the true nature of sex, its value, and the mystery which it embodies.

To understand the nature of spousal love — this glorious heritage of paradise — and the God-willed valid aspect of the sexual sphere, we should read the Song of Solomon with an open mind. We should not think of the analogical meaning, but take it in its original literal sense. Then we can breathe the atmosphere of this love and see the sublimity of the bodily union when experienced as the ultimate God-given mutual self-donation.

And once we have grasped the beauty of the literal sense, we should consider the implications of the fact that the Liturgy uses it as an analogy for the relation of the soul to God.

Is it not obvious that only something which is noble on the human level can be used as an analogy for the supernatural relation of the soul to Christ? Why does the sacred author use

---

[1] Song of Sol. 8:7.

this relation and not that of friendship, such as the one uniting David and Jonathan?

Only when we have corrected this wrong attitude toward the love between man and woman — and toward the bodily union in which this love, aspiring to an indissoluble union, finds its unique fulfillment — can we do justice to the meaning and value of marriage as well as to the depth and beauty of its connection with the coming into being of a new human person.

❧

*Man, Woman, and
the Meaning of Love*

Chapter One

❧

The nature of love

To understand the true nature of love and sex, we must first free ourselves from a widespread general prejudice: the belief that the only valid, authentic reality is the one which natural science presents to us. The rest is dismissed as romance.

The laboratory approach to love

Many believe that vibrations are more serious and real than colors or tunes, that the aspect of a human hand under the microscope is the authentic one, and that the aspect of a hand as we see it is a mere semblance. Many believe that it is in the laboratory alone that we touch the valid, authentic reality.

This is a disastrous error which cuts us off from the most important part of reality. It is not only a dull and gray notion of the world; it is simply a wrong one — a deformed, unrealistic one (as every one-sided outlook is).

If one considers the true nature of the love between man and woman — this tremendous reality of which the literature of all countries and all epochs has sung and which found its most glorious expression in the Song of Solomon — to be nothing but a delightful illusion, one is doomed to misunderstand the true nature of this love. In calling it *romance*, one has already accepted the distorted laboratory conception of reality.

We should rather come to see that this love with all its bliss is not a mere romance but a full, true reality; and that the image which the lover has of the beloved is much deeper, truer, and more existential than the insipid image which any non-lover has of another person. Goethe said once of poetry that it is like the stained-glass windows of a church: seen from outside, they look black, dull, and shapeless. But when one enters the church, their whole splendor is revealed. Obviously, the aspect from the inside is the authentic and valid one. This applies to all great and important things which are endowed with true values. As long as we look at them from outside, as long as we approach them with the laboratory attitude, they cannot be grasped in their true nature and meaning.

In claiming that looking at something from without is the realistic approach, one implies that someone does justice to reality only to the extent that he is blunt and insipid, that he grasps the true nature of the universe and all its different beings more realistically than the more awakened, richer person, the differentiated person. Why should the spiritually nearsighted grasp reality more authentically than the one with exceptional sight? No, we have to free ourselves from the superstition that the laboratory approach is the only authentic one.

Love does not begin with self-love
The first prerequisite for attaining a true understanding of the nature of love is to start from love in its literal, authentic

sense, the love for another person, for a *thou* — whether it is the love of a friend for his friend, the love of a mother for her child, the love of a spouse for a spouse, or the love of a person for God. We must start with analysis of the personal act of love and not from abstract, vague analogies of love, such as the desire for self-perfection, which can also be found in impersonal beings.

It is, however, not enough to abstain from vague analogies taken from the impersonal realm; we also must avoid starting with a completely analogous sense of love, such as self-love. We should rather concentrate on love for another person, the fully experienced and accomplished act of loving directed to a *thou*. This is love in the literal sense, which plays such a basic role in man's life and in the literature of all epochs and countries.

By *self-love*, one generally means the ultimate solidarity which man has with himself. Man is by his very nature inevitably interested in his own happiness and welfare. Naturally, he shuns sufferings. But this solidarity is not the result of a love we have for ourselves, not the outcome of a conscious position taken toward ourselves; it is rather necessarily rooted in our nature; it flows out of the ontological unity of the person.

We need not love our own body in order to care when it hurts us, because we feel it in any case; we need not love ourselves in order to resent it when someone offends or mistreats us or to rejoice when we make a profit.

But in order to be concerned about the pains which another person undergoes, we must love her, because these do not inevitably affect us by themselves. When Blessed Jordan of Saxony wrote to Blessed Diana: "I feel in my own leg the pains which you suffer in yours,"[2] then we face an extraordinary love.

But if a person were to say, "I feel pains in my own leg because I broke it," this would in no way be a sign of an extraordinary love for himself. His pain he feels anyway.

The solidarity which we have with another person and which induces us to say: "Your sufferings are my sufferings; your happiness is my happiness," is a result of love, a fruit of love, an achievement of love, of the conscious position taken toward the loved one, of an experienced blissful response to him. But the solidarity with our own happiness and welfare is not the result of love, but rather of our nature, of the unity of our being; it is something inevitable.

This solidarity with ourselves in no way presupposes a response toward ourselves, implying all the features of love such as delight and a unique bliss. Therefore, all attempts to start an analysis of love with the solidarity we experience with ourselves are doomed to miss the true nature of love.

We only need look at cases in which our relation to another person is really based on a prolongation of the solidarity we have with ourselves in order to grasp clearly the radical difference between this kind of interest and love for another person.

Love responds to the value of the beloved
Properly understood, and in the most immediate sense, love is only love to the extent that it concerns another person.

---

[2] *Letter 43* in the Latin edition of B. Altaner.

Whether it is for a child, a parent, or a friend — whether it involves the newly wedded, our love for God, or our love of neighbor — it is always love for someone else. And although love of things which enjoy no personal structure (e.g., a nation, one's homeland, a country, a work of art, a house, etc.) is much nearer to love in the proper sense than self-love is, still it is love only in an analogous sense.

Love is not mere attachment

Similarly, attachment to things, whether it concerns food, drink, money, etc., can never be identified with what we mean by *loving* even in the most analogous sense. A sharp distinction must be made when considering the critical matter of love. A drinker does not *love* alcohol, nor the miser his money. They become attached to these things, of course. They are subjected to their influence and there is an indescribable attraction involved.

But the element of *attachment* one finds in love is of an entirely different kind. The kind of attraction in the one case is so different from what one finds in the other that the analogy is a deceptive one. The danger of such analogies must be kept in mind.

If I begin with the experience of attachment to something, the nature of love will necessarily be misunderstood. That which accounts for what is peculiar to love, its specific nature, rigidly excludes it from every other type of attachment to something else. This difference concerns that which makes a value-response different from a response to what is merely agreeable.

Moreover, a gap exists between the delight which is occasioned by value and the delight which is not so occasioned.

An example of the former would be the enjoyment one experiences in visiting a beautiful place. The beauty of the scenery and thus its value, accounts for its attraction and delight.

The pleasures taken in a warm bath or the diversion provided by a game of cards, however, are examples of enjoyment which does not depend upon value. In these cases there is no value to which I could be expected to give an appropriate response. All that is concerned is the quality of pleasure which, when it is legitimate, makes something *become objectively good for me*. The fact that certain foods taste good to me or that a card game is enjoyable hinges upon something of this sort. Every sort of attachment to things of this type — things which are agreeable in the widest sense of the word without having a value of their own or without being enjoyable on the basis of value — is essentially different from the attachment to real things whose enjoyment is due to their value.

It should be strongly emphasized that there is considerable danger in trying to assess the nature of love by introducing analogies from a dimension where delight is not based on value and in which one's attitude toward the thing is based on something else altogether.

Love is not merely a means to happiness

If we proceed in such a way, we arrive at the unhappy notion that the person who is loved functions as a means toward our happiness. Purely pleasurable things, things satisfying to self, can of course be considered means to one's pleasure. But this is altogether impossible where delight is due to a thing's value. My concern for such things must be for their own sake. In this way alone can they bring me untold happiness. This is especially true in the case of love. There is no more basic misunderstanding of love than the idea that it involves the surrender of oneself to another person in order to achieve happiness.

Affirmation of the other person as such is what takes place in love. My own desire for happiness can never give rise to love for him. But happiness does come from union with another because of the love I bear him. Happiness is love's outcome, never its motive. Where someone is loved he is an end in himself and certainly not a means toward something else. It is therefore of love's essence, wherever it is found, that the loved one seem precious, beautiful, and worthy of love. Where a human being is no more than useful, where nothing more than good use can be made of him, there is not even a chance for love's beginning. Whether it is a question of love for one's child, parents, friend, or spouse, the surrender which is found in each instance of love presupposes the loved one's full worth, his beauty, and his being precious — in a word, his being worthy of love in an objective sense. Love is a *value-response*.

Love affirms the person of the beloved
No doubt Aristotle saw that true friendship is possible only on the basis of value considerations. Only then does one's interest aim at another person as a person. Where this takes place, the responsiveness to value, which is typical of love,

stands out clearly. This inherent responsiveness in love's interest is directed essentially to the other person as a person. His existence, together with his whole being, is fully thematic. But insofar as someone is merely useful, a source of diversion or amusement, he is not in himself thematic. And he is not loved.

The values considered here and the delight which flows from them must be such that they have some connection with the person as person. He must be fully thematic. If, for example, someone is of an altogether poetic and charming nature and there is something enchanting in his life's rhythm, these values are such that they make the person precious and beautiful. In one's enjoyment of these values, the person remains fully thematic. This is especially the case where the value in question is a spiritual orientation which shines through his personality, revealing his charm and attraction. Value of this kind is, of course, part of a person as person. And every attempt to use him as a means for enjoying his spiritual endowment is bound to be frustrated, for the charm would immediately dissolve. These values are such that they make the person precious and beautiful. In one's enjoyment of these values, the person remains fully thematic. This is all the more true where moral and religious values are concerned. Where another's generosity, purity, goodness, deep religious faith, or love of Christ are the attraction, these values are so much a part of what he is that, in actually adorning him, they make him fully thematic. And one's awareness is turned in a special way to him as a person. The delectableness flows here univocally from this person's preciousness and lovableness.

Love invariably includes, in each of its forms, an awareness that the loved one is precious as well as the presence of value which is so much a part of him personally that his full worth as a person becomes beautifully apparent. His immeasurable worth and beauty account for everything attractive and delightful in him.

The thing of crucial import in this connection is that there is, in every instance of love, a characteristic response to value. This type of surrender to the other cannot be separated from the fact that he is precious, beautiful, and worthy of love.

When we are confronted by the question as to why we love someone, we cannot, by way of explanation, list his worthwhile qualities as we would make up a tally. But this fact should not result in any confusion about love's responsiveness to value.

There are, in the first place, of course, more qualitative values than there are notions of them. And there are more kinds of value than we can name. Where love is concerned, however, it is a question primarily of an individual person's beauty taken as a whole, and of his excelling worth. This has to do with something central, a datum of worth, which is actually supplied by many vital, spiritual, and moral values. This datum can never be reduced to such values, nor ever be formulated as they can. But this is because a person's overall beauty cannot be classified.

Where one loves a friend, the central datum of worth — namely his preciousness as a unique individual — is especially clear. And this is even more true in the case of the love of spouses for each other. What gives rise to love or to the great sense of joy taken in another person is the beauty and preciousness of his individual personality, taken in its fullness. We could call it the beauty of the special divine idea which this person embodies.

But the fact that one cannot readily account for his love by having recourse to such things as the other's reliability, uprightness, intelligence, or spiritual integrity is in no way prejudicial to love's character as value-response. Instead, this accounts for the deep and central presence of value which love presupposes. Love's character as responsiveness to value is revealed even as our awareness is directed to the presence of a special type of value.

⁂

Love is not an appetite

There remains yet another misunderstanding which must be corrected. Wherever love is taken for an appetite or a craving, wherever it is considered some kind of spiritual force which corresponds to desire on the physical plane, the essence of love is radically contradicted.

Where this is done, the loved one's beauty and his attractiveness is mistakenly reduced to the capacity for satisfying desire. Such a mistake has bearing not only on the understanding of love, but also on the entire sphere of man's responses. Further, this involves not only a misunderstanding of value-response, but — what is worse — a misunderstanding of value itself. I have gone into this in my book *Christian Ethics*.[3]

---

[3] *Ethics* (Chicago: Franciscan Herald Press, 1972).

The nature of love

There are attitudes in man which are immanently grounded in his nature, such as, for instance, all kinds of needs. Needs, of course, play a significant role in one's life. The important thing to note is that they are not engendered by the object of the need and its importance. Instead, they come to the fore spontaneously. An object is sought, so to speak, which can bring about appeasement of a need.

But in the case of responses — and more especially in all value-responses — it is the object and its importance which brings to life the attitude of responsiveness in a person. Where need is involved, demand itself is actually the determining factor (*principium*), and it is the object that is determined (*principiatum*).

But where response is involved, the object determines and the person's attitude is determined. Every need, of course, has its origin in human nature and, in this case, an object has importance just as long as the need is present. The importance which it may possess of itself is not a factor. In this way the peculiar importance that an object has for a person is built up: it is capable of satisfying a need. But if the need, the drive, the appetite should disappear, the object which was itself once attractive would cease to be so altogether. Nor would it retain any importance.

The decisive thing which differentiates an appetite from a value-response lies in the fact that, for the latter, the object's importance does not consist in the satisfaction of personal need, whether it be subjective or objective need. Instead the object is *important-in-itself*. Where response to value is involved, the value of the thing is itself the end; in the case of appetite, however, there is a question of a need satisfied or, in other words, of something which the subject requires as necessary to its fulfillment.

There is a second difference between an appetite and an interest in an object because of its value. Value evokes a response to that which is important-in-itself. The object's value actually calls the response into being. Appetite, however, is aroused by one's make-up. An object arrests one's attention because it has within itself the power of satisfying a need — because it is *needed*. It is for this reason (and not because of any value of its own), that the object is *an objective good*.

Love is the voice of the heart

Another old and deep-rooted prejudice is the view that what comprises the affective sphere is not really spiritual in nature. The supposition that only intellect and will are part of man's spiritual nature and that the entire realm of emotions (commonly called *the heart*) belongs to purely vital and irrational components of man is a remnant of Greek intellectualism. But this view has never been proven, nor can it claim to be evident.

For unbiased analysis of the emotions shows that meaningful responses to value (e.g., joy, mourning, respect, and admiration) display all the marks of spiritual activity found, for example, in knowledge, conviction, presumption, and willing. As soon as one grasps that full emotional expression is not incompatible with spiritual activity and that in man there are three spiritual centers (intellect, will, and heart — as Haecker has shown[4]), there is no longer any reason for adhering to an interpretation of love that makes it into an act of the will, as frequently but unfortunately happens. Formerly it was thought necessary to turn love into an act of the will to preserve its spirituality. But love is, clearly and beyond doubt, a response of the heart. Obviously neither the love of a Jonathan for David, nor of a St. Monica for St. Augustine, nor the love of a Leonore for Florestan in Beethoven's *Fidelio*, are an act of willing. Spousal love (as is so admirably described in the Song of Solomon) or the love of St. Paul for his followers (whom he calls "my joy and my crown"[5]) are clearly something other than an act of willing.

Love clearly differs from that extraordinary act which is at the basis of all our actions — namely willing — an act directed toward the realization of a state of affairs not yet real, the act through which we intervene in the world. No, indeed, love is univocally a voice of the heart, an affective response. If love were really an act of willing, how could St. Paul say: "And if I distribute all my goods to feed the poor, and deliver my body to be burnt, yet I do not have charity, it profits me nothing."[6]

Love is different from other affective responses
We must now ask: what distinguishes love from other affective responses involving value (e.g., esteem, admiration,

---

[4] Theodor Haecker, *Metaphysik des Fühlens* (Munich: Kösel-Verlag, 1950).

[5] Phil. 4:1.

[6] 1 Cor. 13:3.

enthusiasm, or veneration)? In accord with what we have mentioned previously, we want to place special emphasis upon the following fact: love typically gives rise to responsiveness regarding the beauty of a very specific individual taken as a whole rather than for values taken individually. Since there is no such thing as loving someone to a certain extent, we cannot love another only to the degree that he has certain qualities. Although it is possible to appreciate him for his learning, I thereby do not have to esteem him as a person.

Similarly, one can be admired for his singing and not his intellectual talent. But since love involves response to another person's beauty taken as a whole because it uniquely embraces the individual as a whole and is at the same time aimed at him as an individual, there can be no love *secundum quid*.

Despite the important role values play, an individual is never merely a bearer of them. He is a real, complete person who can never be replaced by any other. If it were possible to conceive of someone who perfectly duplicated another person's potential and value in every way — something which is altogether untenable — one of the two would still be the one loved and there would never be a desire to exchange him for the other. Where there is love, the incomparable fullness of an individual's meaning as a human person is intimately involved.

ॐ

Love yearns for union

Basic orientation toward achieving union (*intentio unionis*) and the desire for doing good (*intentio benevolentiae*) are the two fundamental or essential characteristics of love whereby it is distinguished from every other instance of friendly or affective responsiveness to value. Consideration will be given first to the *intentio unionis*. Where there is love, there is yearning for spiritual union with the beloved. There is longing not simply for the other's presence, for knowledge of him in his life, joys, and sorrows. There is, even more, a yearning for the union of hearts which mutual love alone can bestow.

However much this yearning for a true union of hearts is uniquely present in married love, both as regards the union and the desire itself, it is still present in a special way wherever love is found.

Love always yearns to be returned. Where there is love of neighbor, there is also a desire that he might feel the need to return that love; and both are involved in the tremendous union which makes up Christ's community of love — and all this is, of course, for His sake. In every love, I move, as it were, spiritually toward the beloved in order to *meet* him; in every love we find this gesture of *hurrying* toward the loved one.

Love does not only exhibit this inclination for union. By means of love, union is achieved — at least to the extent that this is possible from the side of the one who loves. Actual union takes place, of course, only when love is returned, when there is a mutual impulse or movement drawing one toward the other. But one person's love is, by itself, already an essential factor in arriving at union. Love not only has this inclination for union, it is also in itself a power for union (*virtus unitiva*). Love yearns for a union which can make love's response take place. But insofar as lies within its power, love actually arrives at union. The twofold aspect of love is most important.

Man, Woman, and the Meaning of Love

But the role of love in achieving union is not limited to the strong movement toward the beloved. It also consists in one's opening up of himself and sharing his spiritual life with the other, an occurrence which takes place in love alone.

Where it does happen, one removes the visor, so to speak, which has up until then hidden and protected his most intimate and inner self. Where there is love, and there alone, one allows such access to himself that genuine *giving* of himself, from the deepest recesses of his being, takes place. Of course, all this is especially characteristic of spousal love, and in a unique way. But there is something similar in every love, even if found only in the degree befitting its own specific type.

Love desires happiness for the beloved

The *intentio benevolentiae* of love is a yearning to make the other person happy. It is genuine concern primarily for his happiness, his success, his well-being. It involves a very special interest in what is of importance to the other person: his happiness and his destiny.

Although the yearning for personal happiness is not, of course, a sign of self-love, it is obviously a disposition of human nature which cannot be ignored. That another person's happiness should be of much concern, however, is not at all obvious, but is exclusively a consequence of love. Still, it is neither separate from nor merely occasioned by love. This at-oneness is produced by love as belonging to its own life and development. Such deep interest in the other's happiness, therefore, cannot really be considered apart from love.

But the *intentio benevolentiae* is also more than a simple longing to make the loved one happy. It is more than genuine interest in his well-being and happiness. As an attitude, it reveals one's disposition of warmth toward the other. It is the breath of goodness emanating from love itself which enables us to speak of it as *diffusive*. And so we find here something analogous to what we discovered in the case of love's striving for union. Just as the *intentio unionis* is as much a step toward the actual achievement of union as it is a yearning for it — similarly, the *intentio benevolentiae* is more than just a yearning to make the other happy, more than just an interest in his welfare. It is a breath of goodness, one which makes of itself an altogether unique and priceless gift in the act of loving. Since the *intentio benevolentiae* can only be found in love, it too differs notably from such responses as esteem, admiration, and respect.

In the light of these two essential characteristics — the *intentio unionis* and the *intentio benevolentiae* — it is now clear that love differs from every other positive responsiveness to personal value.

Closely connected with the *intentio unionis* and the *intentio benevolentiae*, of course, are a number of other characteristics of love. Wherever love is found, for example, there is a donation of self. In the case of married love this is so noticeable that it can be spoken of literally as a *donation of oneself*. Where love of God is concerned, one's gift of self extends even farther, in a thoroughly exceptional sense which is yet quite real. But every instance of love includes at least a certain element of donation and giving away of oneself.

But if the *intentio unionis* cannot be understood at all as a yearning for fusion, neither can the donation of self (as *intentio benevolentiae*) be interpreted as an ontological giving of one's self. The individuality of persons is objectively maintained in both cases.[7] Moreover, the fact of individual separateness is maintained subjectively in one's experience. It is actually no less essential to the experience of giving and receiving than it is to the experience of union.

[7] This is so obvious, it hardly needs to be said; for each person is, clearly, an individual by nature. The idea of literal spiritual and bodily fusion with another is, of course, absurd if not impossible.

Chapter Two

⁂

The beauty of love

❧

In loving and in giving of oneself to the beloved, there is no consciousness of renouncing one's character as an individual. Rather, the act of giving makes one to be more truly oneself.

❧

Love perfects the lover

One becomes more totally and authentically alive. One's very own life becomes more awakened, fuller in the existential sense. Mutual awareness of one person for the other is completely and vitally maintained.

What is more, a uniquely full and meaningful subjectivity is achieved in this surrender. Where one can say, "I am yours," there is no *giving up* of oneself. The gift implied in *yours* presupposes that it is the complete living person who belongs to the beloved.

To the extent that we fail to grasp what love really is, it is impossible for us to give adequate philosophical consideration to what man is. Love alone brings a human being to full awareness of personal existence. For it is in love alone that man finds room enough to be what he is.

Man, Woman, and the Meaning of Love

To the extent that we regard or think of a person as just another individual who can be understood in terms of his own self-contained striving, we fall short of grasping what is wholly novel and incomparable in personal being. Man's transcendence, i.e., the ability to come into close relationship and understanding with another being or a *thou*, the capacity for responding to another's value and for becoming interested in him for his own sake, the capacity for laying hold of what lies beyond himself and his own immanent tendencies — these make up what is especially characteristic of personality. And upon them depends the dignity which a person enjoys in rising high above all impersonal being. Even on the natural level, the Lord's saying, "He who loses his soul will find it,"[8] holds good.

Of course, every created person receives personal being as a pure gift from the hand of God. Still, the obligation of continually striving to become more personal rests directly upon the nature of a creation so unique. The great French philosopher Marcel said that being a person involves more than just the bare fact. It is also a conquest.[9]

The same can be said of love. The capacity to love is a gift of God, whether it be the power itself or the ability to love one particular person. At the same time, however, there is an obligation, an appeal to our free will, which involves more than one's characteristic stance of loyalty or steadfastness with

[8] Matt. 16:25.

[9] Gabriel Marcel, *Du refus à l'invocation* (Paris: Gallimard, 1940), 236.

respect to love. It has to do with the fact that in order to really love, one must learn how. We shall touch upon this again at the end of this chapter.

Love sees the true self of the beloved

A representative mark of genuine love is found where each of the other person's worthwhile qualities is looked upon as really his, as typical of him. But his shortcomings are presumed to be unusual deviations from his real self. Where something undesirable is apparent, the expression "That's not like him" is characteristic of love.

In the case of someone whom we do not love, qualitative values and disvalues are accorded the same rank, so to speak. But where there is genuine love in response to the other person's beauty taken as a whole, it is to be expected that his negative traits will not be considered typical. Instead they take on the quality of being out of harmony with his true nature.

Especially noteworthy of love is the way it differs from a neutral or objective attitude toward others. So-called *objective regard* or *impartial estimation* considers a person's positive and negative qualities as equally characteristic of him — both types belong to him. While looking upon positive traits as genuinely or *really* there, love considers everything negative as a deviation — which stands in conflict, unfaithfulness, and denial — from what the other truly is. Such is the unique credit which love, and love alone, grants.

This same credit also plays an important part in love of neighbor. This is how love manages to keep the ontological worth of a person in mind rather than the qualitative values belonging to him as an individual. In this way love responds to God's image (the *imago Dei*) in the other, seeing him in the light of that likeness to God (the *similitudo Dei*) which should one day be his. Far from considering qualitative disvalues as constitutive for his personality, this love sees them as a betrayal of the noble essence of the *imago Dei*.

⚭

Love is never blind

A friend's shortcomings are viewed as contradictory to his true nature. They are neither reckoned as his, nor looked upon as if they were as typical of him as are his good qualities, but this does not imply that one is inclined to overlook them or explain them away. Nor does it pretend that they are any the less plain or noticeable. Love makes us sensitive to faults in another because the beauty of his personality is present to our mind as a whole. And so it is of very great importance to us that he remain wholly faithful to what he most truly is and that his real self become fully manifest.

It is altogether mistaken to think that love is blind. Actually it opens one's eyes. But pride, which one finds so often with love, does make one blind — especially where a loved one is considered an extension of one's own ego. The mother who looks upon her child as an extension of herself believes the child incapable of any faults, of course. But this is typical of pride and not at all of love.

Where there is a question of faults there is naturally a big difference between those which concern someone we love and those of a person we do not love. Faults are irksome in anyone for whom we have little love. They cause us to become irritable and make us indignant. We do not see them against the background of the beauty of his personality taken as a whole. Instead we look at them separately and attribute them to him along with his good qualities.

But when there is a question of someone we love, nothing is irksome. We are not irritated. We are only unhappy for the loved one and for the fact that he has these faults. We grieve at the presence of what is essentially untrue of him, and this we do out of a deep sense of unity with him. In profound awareness of our own weakness and frailty, mindful of how unfaithful we are to ourselves and to what God desires of us, we lovingly face the faults when they occur, meeting each such instance of weakness with empathy, rejecting them inwardly for him and with him.

⁂

Only love is truly objective

Where there is love, our perception of the other's faults is more objective (in the proper sense of the word) than in instances where there is no love whatever. We come to better grips with reality when we see another's failings in the light of his whole personality, understanding them from within, sorrowing over them because of what the loved one is. There is even keen suffering for his sake, not because his faults are a burden but because our love for him makes his inner growth and attaining a perfection a matter of great concern to us.

The kind of credit which love makes possible has a particular nobility about it. One discovers in it the special largesse of love — a value which does not, however, take its origin altogether from the responsive attitude evoked by value. Such conviction, rooted in love's act of giving, involves an element of hope which carries a special blessing for the loved one — a blessing which is also one of love's gifts.

⁂

Love believes

There is, however, still another kind of credit. We refer to what concerns the other's nature in areas which have not yet had the chance of discovery. Love believes only the best of another person. At first it does not even credit to him the undesirable traits that are attributed to him (or it assumes that they were not correctly interpreted).

Consequently, we find that wherever there is love there is also an element of faith. And what has not yet been experienced of the other's beauty is taken into account on the basis of what has been experienced. We are not now concerned with the ordinary sort of confidence which one usually finds in each genuine manifestation of love, as, for example, between friends or in the case of a child's love for his parents. This element of faith consists much more in one's filling out the picture of the beloved in all dimensions not yet known — on the basis of what is completely accessible in his beauty.

Attending this credit is the resolve to interpret everything in the other person positively, so long as nothing in him is clearly suggestive of the contrary.

There are, of course, so many things about a person which can be understood in different ways. There are many things done, said, or concealed which are not definitely moral or immoral in themselves. They are neither beautiful nor ugly, neither stupid nor intelligent. But they are meaningful and fully significant in the light of a given person's background and his whole personality. Even as it is typical of jealous and hateful behavior for one to be ever alert to catch the other in his mistakes, giving a negative interpretation to everything he does, so it is basically characteristic of love to be hopeful of seeing the other adopt a course in accord with what is good, right, and beautiful — a dwelling on God's path. Basic to love, also, is its continual readiness to take everything that could be understood differently in the best possible light. Such willingness to give the other person the benefit of the doubt is closely related to the faithful credit one maintains with respect to the other.

Love always assumes what is best in the other. So long as there is no reason for reckoning with the presence of a fault, love entertains the more favorable opinion toward all that is doubtful. When love encounters a fault in the other, it is like meeting disloyalty or infidelity to what is truest in his nature (and it is never accepted on a par with his positive qualities). This threefold attitude is characteristic of the credit which love — and love alone — grants.

Love is not a delusion
One should not confuse this credit of faith, however, with the inclination to idealize, which is typical of day-dreamers. Generosity, which is typical of love, presupposes the existence

of a corresponding value which justifies and gives it meaning. But where there are only dreams, the central thing is a need to experience delight and to have contact with admirable and extraordinary people. Pleasure of this sort is so strongly desired that one commits himself to an imaginary ideal. One enjoys dreaming. The person one idealizes is more an *occasion for dreaming* than a meaningful subject to be taken seriously in himself. One imagines that everything about the other is splendid and grand, although one has had no opportunity to know him well enough to be certain.

The difference between such an unfounded attitude and the faithful credit of faith of love (to which we have already made reference) is what we shall now consider.

This credit of faith belongs to the gift of love which is itself a value-response. Even though it goes beyond any other value-response, it is not on that account a kind of spontaneous *need* which can somehow be separated from what characterizes love as a value-response. Dreaming, however, is symptomatic of a need — an appetite — that seeks to get as much as it can without having any concern or responsiveness for things of value.

Love surrenders

Love's generous credit is intimately bound up with its surrender. The loving person in no way seeks his own gratification. He is oriented completely toward the other. And his trusting conviction is completely for the other's sake, having nothing whatever of self-gratification about it.

The dream, however, is always for gratification's sake. It does not have the other person in mind, but rather him who dreams.

This credit has nothing of extravagance about it. It goes hand in hand with the realization that a noble man is also quite frail and weak. Where everything seems to be in order, love reckons with the possibility that there may be imperfections which must be faced as unpleasant but temporary facts, even though it will never be prejudiced by them. The loving credit does not dwell in an ethereal or unreal region. It does not mount Pegasus. Rather, it fortifies itself on ground which is altogether real, characterized by holy surroundings.

Nor is the radical difference between loving credit and dreaming fancy somehow diminished by the fact that one can also be disappointed where love is authentic or that credit can sometimes come to real disappointment itself. It is not the possibility of disappointment which makes the dreamer's fancies to be what they are. They are characterized, rather, by the absence of true love, by the ethereal, unreal, and even deceptive atmosphere in which the life of desire is led. One might say that "the lover can be disappointed but the dreamer deceives himself."

This threefold credit is, of course, bearer of a value which is specifically moral. Although it does not exactly come from love's responsiveness, it is rooted in the power of giving which belongs to love.

In the gift of love, what is best in the being of the loving person is brought out. And it is clear that what love's value consists in — its depth, ardor, and nobility — depends to a large extent upon the character of the lover himself and not merely on the values in the other which enkindle his love.

Love must be learned

With Christ as our witness, we should strive continually to be impressed with the greatness and seriousness of love and also with the realization that love is much deeper and more important than most professional activities. This should be noted especially in our day when work so often makes up the only serious side of life and when the quest for amusement and recreation stands in the way of everything else.

But this is possible only if we rescue ourselves from the whirl of activity and the anticipation of the next moment's confusion which deprives us of any full awareness of the present. In other words, it can happen only if we provide a special place for contemplation in our lives.

Only if we strive always to plumb the depths and, in this way, attain to Christ and ultimate reality, can we ever hope to learn how to love truly. Only as we continue to consider the one we love and his love for us as unmerited gifts — and this in deep gratitude, never taking them for granted — can we attain to true love.

One who truly loves is filled with respect and gratitude

Out of such respect and gratitude alone can true love blossom. The human person awakens completely only in love; and it is in love alone that he attains the transcendence to which he is called. St. Augustine tells us that *in loving, man himself becomes worthy of love*. In fact, wherever the transforming power of Christ has touched each of love's manifestations, the person who loves is as a dim but glorious reflection of that of which he attains a fuller share — the fire of which our Lord speaks when he says: "I have come to bring fire upon the earth, and what is my desire but that it should burn?"[10]

[10] Luke 12:49.

Chapter Three

⁂

The grandeur of spousal love

The very meaning and value which marriage possesses of its own cannot be understood if we fail to start from the great and prominent reality of the love between man and woman.

Religion does not overlook the grandeur of spousal love

Here, let us be frank, we touch on a kind of scandal in Catholic writings on marriage. In them, one finds much discussion of the will of the flesh, the remedy for concupiscence, mutual help and assistance, and procreation; but one hears very little of love. We mean the love between man and woman, the deepest source of happiness in human life, the great, glorious love of which the Song of Solomon says: "If a man would give all the substance of his house for love, he would despise it as nothing."[11]

In contradiction to the general silence concerning this love, Pope Pius XII has uttered some eloquent words:

> The charm exercised by human love has been for centuries the inspiring theme of admirable works of

---

[11] Song of Sol. 8:7.

genius, in literature, in music, in the visual arts; a theme always old and always new, upon which the ages have embroidered, without ever exhausting it, the most elevated and poetic variations.[12]

It is unbelievable that the real, valid motive for marriage has been for the most part overlooked and the intrinsic relation of this type of love to a full mutual self-donation in the bodily union is ignored. Compared with this great, noble, basic incentive, which the Song of Solomon says "is stronger than death,"[13] the isolated desire of the flesh is superficial and secondary.

Who can deny that it is this love which shakes the soul of man to its very depths, which marks the deepest experience in human life? Certainly, there is a broad scale in the love potential of men, in the depth, the completeness of love. Leonardo da Vinci said: "The greater the man, the deeper his love." Great loves such as St. Elizabeth of Hungary and her husband, or St. Louis of France and his wife, may be rare and presuppose great and deep personalities; but in every human being who has ever experienced a real love — limited and imperfect as it may be — it is the great, dynamic human experience in his life.

It is unbelievable how the great and serious thing which is love between man and woman is dealt with sometimes in sermons. One can hear that this love is nothing but a romance which should play no role in marriage, that it is only the will that matters, the observance of moral commandments, the duties implied in marriage.

[12] *The Pope Speaks* (New York: Pantheon, 1957), 21.
[13] Song of Sol. 8:6.

The grandeur of spousal love

We shall never be able to understand the grandeur and depth of marriage if we do not first grasp the beauty, grandeur, and seriousness of the love, whose nature is nowhere so adequately rendered as in the Song of Solomon.

It cannot be stated with sufficient emphasis that the time has come for us to do away with the gnostic and puritanical tendency to be suspicious of spousal love.

Let us be existential: let us see that the love between man and woman is a specific category and type of love, that it is a beautiful and glorious reality which is destined by God's will to play a fundamental role in man's life, that this love is the classical motive for marriage, and that marriage is precisely the fulfillment of this love.

Spousal love and differences between men and women

The special character of spousal love is marked by the fact that this love can only exist between men and women but not between persons of the same sex (as is the case with friendship, parental love, and filial love). Yet it would be incredibly superficial to consider the difference between men and women to be merely biological; in fact, we are confronted with two complementary types of the spiritual person of the human species.

Men and women differ essentially

The difference between man and woman must not be overrated nor underrated. Sometimes it has been grossly overrated (as, for instance, by Aristotle when he stated that man was a

Man, Woman, and the Meaning of Love

being in act, and woman a *being in potency*[14]). Also, in the course of many centuries, custom has applied different moral standards to the conduct of men and to that of women. This is quite wrong. There is but one moral law for both and both are equally full human persons. Human nature is identical in both.

On the other hand, one must not underrate and reduce the difference between men and women to mere biology. There exist without any doubt such things as specific feminine or masculine features of the personality. Much as some feminists try to deny or at least minimize the existence of sex-based personal characteristics, much as many modern women are eager to efface this difference in adapting their demeanor to that of men, the difference in the personality structure of man and woman remains an undeniable reality.

If we try to delineate these specifically feminine and masculine features, we find in women a unity of personality by the fact that heart, intellect, and temperament are much more interwoven, whereas in man there is a specific capacity to emancipate himself with his intellect from the affective sphere. This unity of the feminine type of human person displays itself also in a greater unity of inner and exterior life, in a unity of style embracing the soul as well as the exterior demeanor. In a woman, the personality itself is more in the foreground than objective accomplishments; whereas man, who has a specific creativity, is more called than she is to objective accomplishments.

Perhaps no one in literature has succeeded so well in showing the specific beauty of femininity as Shakespeare. Whether

[14] Aristotle, *On the Generation of Animals,* Bk. 1, 729b14.

we think of Cordelia, Rosalind, Desdemona, Viola, Ophelia, or Portia, in each character the very nature of femininity in all its specific beauty deploys itself before our eyes.

What matters in our context is to understand, first, that man and woman differ not merely in a biological and physiological direction, but that they are *two different expressions of human nature*; and, second, that the existence of this duality of human nature possesses a great value. Even if we prescind for the moment from all biological reasons as well as from procreation, we must see how much richer the world is because this difference exists, and that it is in no way desirable to efface as much as possible this difference in the spiritual realm, a trend which is unfortunately very widespread today.

Man and woman are complementary

It is also important to see that this difference has a specifically complementary character. Man and woman are spiritually oriented toward each other; they are created for each other. First, they have a mission for each other; second, because of their complementary difference, a much closer communion and more ultimate love is possible between them than between persons of the same sex.

Their mutual mission manifests itself in a wholesome mutual enrichment as well as in the mitigation of the dangers to which the masculine and the feminine type of human beings are exposed when they are deprived of this influence. The positive enriching influence displays itself in an inspiring tension, in a fecundation on a purely spiritual level.

Man, Woman, and the Meaning of Love

Concerning the mitigation of dangers, we can easily see how men are in danger of becoming coarse, dried out, or depersonalized by their office and profession when they are completely cut off from any contact with the feminine world. And women are in danger of becoming petty, self-centered, and hypersensitive when they are completely cut off from all contact with men. It is therefore a great bliss for the child, be it male or female, that it receives the influence of both father and mother.

This difference between man and woman is an enormous enrichment of our earthly existence. The world is more colorful and life more attractive for men because there are women and for women because there are men. Women have for men (and vice versa) a specific charm extending from the soul to the bodily appearance, which is based on objective values and a being ordered toward the opposite sex.

But this wholesome mutual influence, this enrichment of the universe resulting from the complementary difference of man and woman, can only unfold if an atmosphere of respect and of mutual reverence reigns between them. Only if a certain distance is maintained (which only in the case of marriage is given up, without however giving up the respect and reverence) can this mutual enrichment take place. It is fulfilled only if one is aware of the mystery which exists in this being ordered toward the opposite. As soon as a kind of humdrum comradeship dominates the relation between the two sexes, as soon as one no longer feels that the very presence of a person belonging to the other sex imposes a different demeanor on us, or as soon as the relation to the other sex is pervaded by self-indulgence and a descent to extramarital sensuality, we necessarily become blind to the gift of this duality; we are blunted to it.

⨏

The characteristics of spousal love

It is not possible to overemphasize the fact that the difference between man and woman is not a merely biological one, but extends also deep into the realm of personality. We must come to see that because of this complementary influence, a specific type of love is possible only between them. This specific love is characterized by a number of marks.

First, it tends toward an *I-thou communion* more than any other love. Elsewhere, I have distinguished two basic dimensions of communion with other persons: *I-thou communion* and *we communion*.[15] In an *I-thou communion*, we are, as it were, in front of the other person and we look at each other. In the *we communion*, on the contrary, we look together with the other person at some object. We rejoice together over something; we accomplish something together. (In this situation we are not, as it were, in front of the other person, but rather we stand next to the other person, hand in hand.)

These two dimensions are *both* to be found in every lasting relationship to another person, according to the situation. But it is also characteristic for one of these dimensions to dominate a relationship, whether the *I-thou* or the *we communion* is typical for a particular case. Spousal love tends in a unique way toward the *I-thou communion*.

[15] *Metaphysik der Gemeinschaft* (Augsburg, 1930), ch. 2.

A second mark, closely linked with the first, is that the spousal beloved is more thematic than in any other love. He has become the great theme of my life; I am focused on him. This expresses itself also in the fact that the *intentio unionis* which is common to all categories of love assumes here not only its highest *tension*, but also extends much farther than in any other love. We long for union with his very being; we long for a common life with him, and the requital of our love assumes an incomparable importance.

The liberating power of spousal love

Spousal love differs especially from all other categories of love by an ecstatic character which one calls *being in love*. Being in love — this being enchanted, being fascinated, being captured by something greater than we are — is often looked at with a smile and considered as an intoxication or an infatuation, a kind of youthful lunacy. This is a great error. In reality, the true state of being in love is a blissful, awakened condition of the soul. One is more awakened for the entire world of values; one lives in a more authentic sense, as Plato has described so admirably in *Phaedrus*.[16]

Certainly there is here, as anywhere, the difference between a deep, true being in love, forming the climax of a deep spousal love, and a superficial infatuation, an ungenuine being in love. This difference exists everywhere. There is true artistic genius and sham genius; there is a true philosopher such as

[16] Plato, *Phaedrus*, 251.

Plato and a sham philosopher such as Sartre. But the possibility of a sham neither affects the value of art or philosophy nor the value of being in love.

In order to see that the truly being in love is something great and noble, we have only to realize how much more beautiful a human being becomes when a great love and a state of being in love fills his heart.

As soon as a man experiences true, real love — the blissful adventure that every love is — we find that he breaks through the network of self-centeredness, that he is widened, and that he pierces through his own pettiness. Indeed, it is in loving alone that one can truly live. Suddenly the lover ceases to be dominated by conventions and conventional values; he is freed from the fetters of what *one does*; he no longer lives as a *one*, but as a real person.

He awakens to the true hierarchy of goods and values; and above all in loving, every man becomes more humble. Even the most mediocre person ceases to be mediocre as soon as he really loves.

I remember a young man who was a nice person but who was plodding along a conventional path, preoccupied with public opinion, imprisoned in conventional categories. He fell in love with a charming woman; it was a deep and genuine love. He did not yet know whether she would requite his love, but suddenly everything was changed in him. He came to see me and said to me that he could no longer understand how he could have lived as he had lived before, in such a mediocre, humdrum manner. The meaning of man's existence had revealed itself to him, the nature of true happiness, and the secondary importance of exterior things such as his career. It is difficult to express how much greater, wider, deeper, and more lovable he had become by loving.

I also recall the case of a friend who was a wonderful person, in no way conventional or mediocre; yet he was too much possessed by his profession as a lawyer and was therefore in danger of making his work the center of his life. He told me that when the woman he deeply loved told him that she loved him in return, he exclaimed: "My office will have to play second fiddle from now on!"

Again, there was this blissful awakening to the true hierarchy of values, this liberation, this generosity of love. For indeed in true love, one attains an inner freedom; in giving ourselves to a *thou,* in transcending our self-centeredness, we attain a blissful freedom.

Through a real love, man is drawn to his depth. His relation to the entire world becomes different, more authentic, and deeper.

Spousal love aims at an irrevocable gift of self

Spousal love is a definite type of love and has a character of its own, even if we prescind from the sphere of sex. Sex is not the *forma* of love. It would be a fundamental error to believe that spousal love is a combination of friendship, love, and sex.

It is true that the special character of conjugal love is marked by the fact that this love can come into being only between men and women, and not between persons of the same sex (as is the case with friendship and parental or filial love). It would be quite wrong, however, to reduce this characteristic to the sexual sphere and to say that conjugal love is just friendship plus sexual relations, presupposing a difference of sex.

Spousal love aims at a full and irrevocable self-donation, at an indissoluble union in the sacred bond of marriage. Only when full justice is done to the nature and value of this love can one grasp the meaning which marriage as a love union already possesses in itself (apart from its primary end, procreation) and that the value which it possesses does not exclusively derive from this end.

We must thus start with an understanding of the meaning and value of marriage as the closest love union between man and woman, as constituting the most intimate human *I-thou communion,* the irrevocable bond which Christ has elevated to a sacrament.

This union is constituted itself by the consent of the spouses, a mutual self-donation for their entire lives, made by the express will of the partners, solemnly pronounced before God, thereby entrusting this bond to God. The *intentio unionis* of spousal love finds its valid expression in this consent and it finds its fulfillment in the irrevocable union constituted by the consent. It reaches, however, a new fulfillment in the conjugal act, in the consummation of the self-donation initiated and promised in the consent. The character of indissolubility begins with the consummation of the marriage, with the fully accomplished self-donation, whereby "they shall be two in one flesh."[17] Who can fail to grasp the grandeur and beauty of

[17] Gen. 2:24.

marriage and the bodily union which it essentially implies if he contemplates without prejudice the words of the Lord in which He refers to the indissolubility of marriage?

Because of the hardness of your heart he wrote you that precept. But from the beginning of creation God made them male and female. For this cause a man shall leave his father and mother, and cleave to his wife, and they shall be two in one flesh. Therefore now they are not two, but one flesh. What therefore God has joined together, let no man put asunder.[18]

Sacramental marriage transforms love

It is not possible within the framework of this book to broach the most sublime aspect of marriage as a sacrament. But we wish to stress that spousal love is also called to be transformed by Christ; indeed, only in Christ and through Christ can the spouses live up to the full glory and depth to which this love in its very nature aspires. As Pius XII has stated:

But what new and unutterable beauty is added to this love of two human hearts, when its song is harmonized with the hymn of two souls vibrating with supernatural life! Here, too, there is a mutual exchange of gifts; and then, through bodily tenderness and its healthy joys, through natural affection and its impulses, through a spiritual union and its delights, the two beings who

[18] Mark 10:5-9.

love each other identify themselves in all that is most intimate in them from the unshaken depths of their beliefs to the highest summit of their hopes.[19]

The transformation of spousal love by Christ does not, however, make it lose its specific character as spousal love. To quote the late Pontiff again: "Where love is transformed, have no fear that it may somehow lose what there is in it of splendor, ardor, or self-surrender. The supernatural does not destroy or alter what is natural. On the contrary, it glorifies it and brings it to perfection."

Limited space allows me but one example as an illustration. The *intentio unionis* is impressed upon married love in a special way. It consists in a striving toward complete oneness of hearts which ought to find its expression in bodily union. But as long as there is no encountering of the other in Christ, there is no going beyond this first step. One can never reach the other completely. The reason for this is the fact that Christ alone has the key to the deepest and most secret recesses of the soul.

In bringing to mind the *intentio benevolentiae*, are we not struck by the realization of how weak and helpless we are whenever we yearn to make the other person happy? We can only look on and do nothing when he is suffering or sick, or when he is dying. But what possibilities are open to us when we place him in the Heart of Jesus, when we entrust him to Christ, when we love him together with Christ, when we realize fully that Christ loves him infinitely more than we do.

[19] *The Pope Speaks*, 21.

Man, Woman, and the Meaning of Love

And finally, love such as this yearns for unlimitedness. We see this especially in the love of the married. Yet how restricted we are, how dreadfully hemmed in by our nature at every turn. This desire for unlimitedness can be fulfilled in Christ alone — to the extent that we participate in and have a share in His infinite love.

It seems to me that every Christian should see creation — the great and mysterious natural good, which also reflects God's glory and contains a message of God — in its deepest meaning and value, and in the splendor which it receives through its transfiguration in Christ.

A pedestrian approach to the goods of creation — be it the beauty of nature, be it man as such, created after the image of God, be it friendship, be it love, be it marriage — seems to me a betrayal, a refusal to testify to the new light which Christ has shed on the entire creation.

It was said that Christians are to be recognized by the fact that they love one another.[20] I would add: Christians should also be recognized by the fact that they who have received the festival clothes in Baptism shun any superficial, mediocre approach to the great goods of creation, that they understand more profoundly than others "how admirable are thy works, O God."[21]

[20] John 13:35.
[21] Ps. 92:5.

Chapter Four

The sublimity of sexual union in marriage

❧

Spousal love aspires to a union which extends much farther than that of simple friendship, filial love, or parental love. It desires a bodily union. In spousal love, the body of the beloved assumes a unique charm as the vessel of this person's soul, and also as embodying in a unique way the general charm and attraction which femininity has for man, or virility has for woman. Spousal love aspires to the bodily union as a specific fulfillment of the total union, as a unique, deep, mutual self-donation. If someone loves another person with spousal love, he realizes the mystery of the bodily union and he aspires to it, because he loves the other person.

Here the bodily disposition for sex, the sensuality in a positive sense, is clearly grasped in its serving function. Its real meaning is to be an expression of spousal love and a fulfillment of the desired union. So in the drama of the German poet Kleist, the lover says: "I do not mind dying if only I have been allowed to be united with my beloved on our wedding night."

A world yawns between the aspect of this bodily union for the real lover and the aspect which it offers as a mere satisfaction of an isolated sexual desire. For the lover, the beloved person is the theme; the most intimate and deep union with her is the primary desire, and all the charm and delight which the sexual sphere embodies, the attraction of femininity, is indissolubly linked to union with the beloved person. In the case of the lover, all the charm of femininity in general actualizes itself in the individuality of the beloved.

In contrast, when someone is animated merely by isolated sexual desire, the partner is an anonymous bearer of the general attraction of femininity. Moreover, the charm of femininity is thereby also reduced to a superficial, physical one. The personality of the partner plays no decisive role; she is exchangeable provided she belongs to the other sex. As Leporello says in Mozart's *Don Giovanni*, "*Purchè porti la gonella!*" ("If only she wears a skirt!")[22]

In the case of the lover, it is exclusively this unique, unduplicable individual personality which embodies the general charm in all its psycho-physical plenitude and depth. It is only against the background of this beloved personality that this charm is fully unfolded. This charm can only fully blossom in the beloved's personality, as Petrarch so beautifully said of Laura: "*Che sola a me par donna*" ("To me, she alone embodies femininity").[23] And vice versa: the woman who loves sees in her beloved all the charm of masculinity.

For the lover, the beloved person is the theme, the most intimate and deep union with him is the primary desire; and all

---

[22] Mozart, *Don Giovanni*, Act I, Aria: "*Madamina, il catalogo è questo.*"

[23] Petrarch, Poem 126, "*Chiare, fresche et dolci acque*" ("Cool, limpid, lovely stream").

the charm and delight which the sexual sphere embodies, the attraction of the opposite sex, is indissolubly linked to the union with the beloved person.

Here the other person is fully seen *as person*. In the case where someone aspires to the satisfaction of a mere isolated sexual desire, the other person is in no way thematic as person; a union with him as a person is in no way sought; he is rather used as an instrument for appeasing a desire or at least as a mere partner in a pleasurable game.

The extraordinary depth of sexuality

If we approach the sphere of sex phenomenologically, if we look at it without prejudice, we cannot but see that it differs completely from all other instincts or appetites. It has a kind of depth which neither thirst nor hunger nor the need to sleep nor any desire for other bodily pleasure possesses.

Whether the charm of the opposite sex affects one as spousal desire or as mere sexual lust, sex acts upon our personal life in a completely different way than other instincts do. Sex has a mysterious character, something irradiating in our psychical life which is found neither in the desire to eat nor in the pleasure which the satisfaction of this desire procures. The sexual ecstasy, especially, goes to the very depth of our bodily existence; in its overwhelming power it is something extraordinary, something to which only terrible bodily pains are a counterpart.

As a result, it is characteristic of sex that in virtue of its very significance and nature, it tends to become incorporated with experiences of a higher order that are purely psychological and spiritual. Nothing in the domain of sex is so self-contained as are other bodily experiences such as eating and drinking. The unique profundity of sex is sufficiently shown by the fact that a man's attitude toward it is of incomparably greater significance for his personality than his attitude toward the other bodily appetites.

୫

The profound intimacy of sexuality

But the sphere of sex has also a character of intimacy which no other instincts have, not even great bodily pains (which share some of its character of depth). In a certain sense, sex is the secret of the individual. Every disclosure of sex is the revelation of something intimate and personal; it is a glimpse into our secret.

Those characteristics of sex are thrown into relief as soon as someone falls in love in the true and authentic sense of the word. In aspiring to bodily union with the beloved, he clearly grasps the unique intimacy of this sphere. By the very fact that he desires above all to reach this union with the beloved, he acknowledges univocally the intimacy and depth of this sphere, and he grasps the exclusivity of this mutual self-donation.

The real attraction of this sphere, its character of something extraordinary, its fascination, is indissolubly linked to its intimate and secret character. As soon as one no longer feels shame in projecting this sphere into the public realm, as soon as one deals with it as if it were merely a biological problem that can be discussed publicly like any medical problem, one inevitably kills the real charm and the mysterious character which sex possesses.

Sex, by its very essence, is not something neutral. To neutralize it means to miss it, to deprive it of all possible significance for human happiness. In order for it to be the ultimate expression of spousal love and the fulfillment of an ultimate union, sex must be grasped and understood in its character as a mystery.

The unfortunate person who lacks all sensuality and is completely indifferent to this sphere by temperamental disposition will be incapable, once married, of seeing in this union the highest form of self-donation and the climax of a blissful union.

Sex is not merely a biological action

Some Christian authors, in undertaking to praise spousal love, deprive it of its ecstatic ardor, of its splendor and unique *intentio unionis*, thus detaching it consistently from the sexual sphere, from the bodily union; others again look down on spousal love and interpret its ecstatic character, its unique splendor, as a mirage, an illusion. Recently, a famous Christian philosopher in this country even went so far as to claim that this type of love is nothing but a disguised sex instinct, and that only insofar as *agape* exists between the spouses does their relationship deserve to be called authentic love. Most authors, however, ignore the existence of this love entirely, simply omitting it when speaking of marriage.

Still another basic error bars the way to understanding the true meaning and value of marriage. It is possible to approach the sphere of sex in man as a mere subdivision of the realm of instincts and biological urges, as if it had no intrinsic relation to the spiritual sphere (like thirst and the need of sleep, whose meanings are to be found in an extrinsic end which they serve). However, such an approach is bound to hinder an understanding of the true nature and meaning of sex. As soon as we assume that the nature and the meaning of sex in man can be treated as a mere biological reality, we have blinded ourselves to the mystery of the sphere of sex — to the meaning and value which it can have on the one hand, and to the terrible moral evil of impurity on the other.

If sex is really nothing more than a biological instinct such as thirst or hunger, it is incomprehensible why the satisfaction of an instinct implanted in man's nature by God should be something immoral outside of marriage, especially if it led to procreation. To consider the sexual sphere as a subdivision of instincts is to reduce the immorality of impurity to the mere violation of a positive commandment.

The instinctual approach to sexuality destroys love

To approach sex as a mere instinct like hunger and thirst destroys the possibility of the great and deep experience of the bodily union as the fulfillment of an ultimate spousal love and a full self-donation. When I say *destroys*, I do not mean that a person who has this approach may not convert himself later on through a great love and radically change his approach to sex, coming then to understand its deep significance as the ultimate expression of spousal love. But I wish to say that the view of sex as a mere instinct such as hunger and thirst is incompatible with grasping and experiencing its deep, mysterious significance as an expression of ultimate love. As soon as someone who saw in sexual intercourse nothing but a normal satisfaction of an instinct awakens through a great and deep love to a discovery of the real meaning of this sphere, he cannot but deeply regret he ever threw himself away, that he ever desecrated this union.

On the other hand, as long as one sees in the sexual act nothing but a normal satisfaction of an instinct, one cannot understand why the bodily union should be the ultimate expression for something so deep as love, how it could ever be the specific fulfillment of the *intentio unionis*.

This should be clear to everyone who has ever loved deeply. If one has grasped that in the bodily union lies a unique gift of one's secret to the beloved, one cannot but see the horror of abusing it as a mere satisfaction of an instinct, as a means for fun, as a vehement physical pleasure, as an amusing game with a person for whom we shall perhaps no longer care a few days later.

The real lover understands that the bodily union is a mysterious and deep thing, that it is here that he discloses his deep secret exclusively to his beloved and that his beloved discloses her secret to him. It is a very significant and profound fact that the Bible speaks of this bodily union as a *knowing*. This term expresses the intimacy and depth of the disclosure of the secret of the person, the self-donation which this union embodies.

We cannot grasp the mystery embodied in this sphere until we grasp that its deepest meaning consists in being a unique fulfillment of spousal love and its desire for union. We must realize that this sphere is essentially ordained toward the constitution of a lasting, irrevocable union, the union to which spousal love aspires, and which is sanctioned by God.

Only then can we grasp the real sinfulness of every isolation of the satisfaction of sexual desire from the constitution of this God-sanctioned union. Only when we understand that the sexual act implies a mutual, irrevocable self-donation and is by its very nature called and destined to constitute an indissoluble union, can we see the desecration involved in sexual satisfaction outside of marriage.

⸙

Conjugal love is not lust

The approach to the sexual sphere as something which constitutes in itself a primary reality, an autonomous sphere, a subdivision of the sphere of instincts, is unfortunately not restricted to Freud. In a completely different form we find this error in every conception of the sexual desire which sees in it primarily an expression of concupiscence, the lust of the flesh, an evil which is at best tolerated when serving the end of procreation and when legitimated in marriage.

In this conception, also, the meaning and value of the sexual sphere is completely overlooked because it is severed from its mission to constitute a unique, irrevocable union between two persons to which the love of man and woman aspires and in which it finds its fulfillment. To quote Pope Pius XII:

> The conjugal act, in its natural structure, is a personal action, a simultaneous and immediate cooperation of

husband and wife, which, owing to the very nature of the agents and the propriety of the act, is the expression of the reciprocal gift which, according to the word of Scripture, effects the union "in one flesh."[24]

We could also apply to the conjugal act the admirable words of St. Ambrose in speaking of the kiss: "Those who kiss one another are not content with the donation of their lips, but must breathe their very souls into each other."[25]

We must, finally, free ourselves from seeing in the bodily union something evil, for whose actualization in marriage one must desperately try to find a reason which can explain why this evil may be tolerated in marriage. We must learn to see that the bodily union, destined to be the fulfillment of spousal love and an ultimate mutual self-donation, is as such something noble and a great mystery, a sacred land which we should approach with deep reverence and never without a specific sanction of God. Precisely because of this nobility and sacred mystery, because of the great value which it is destined to realize, every abuse is a terrible sin and even contains something sacrilegious.

Isolated sexuality threatens love

While stressing that it is a grave error to see the sexual sphere and the sexual act as something evil as such, we also

[24] *The Pope Speaks*, 27.
[25] St. Ambrose, *Book on Isaac and the Soul*, Bk. 1, ch. 3.8.

acknowledge that isolation of the sexual sphere is not only a theoretical error but a widespread tendency of our fallen nature. When isolated and separated from spousal love and the mutual self-donation in marriage, the sexual sphere has an enormous attractive power. The danger of being caught and seduced by this aspect of the sexual sphere is indeed a great one and it lurks in the greater part of mankind. My book *In Defense of Purity* deals at length with this powerful fascination. Wherever anyone gives in to it and undertakes to satisfy an isolated sexual desire, we are confronted with the grave sin of impurity, an outgrowth of evil concupiscence and a desecration. This sin includes a mysterious betrayal of our spiritual nature. But this in no way entitles us to look at the act of bodily union as something evil. It becomes evil through its isolation.

Precisely because it is something noble, deep, and mysterious in its God-ordained relation to two becoming one flesh in the sublime love union of marriage, its abuse is a terrible desecration. To conclude that something is evil as such because its abuse constitutes a terrible sin and because in our fallen nature the tendency for such abuse is great, is obviously completely illogical. Should we look on intellectual work and scholarship as something evil in itself, because it certainly produces in many persons a proud attitude, because it fosters pride? Is St. Peter Damian right when claiming that the Devil is the father of grammar because he taught us to decline God in the plural: *Eritis sicut dii?*[26] Should we extend to all men the ban laid by

---

[26] Peter Damian, *On holy simplicity*, 1.

The sublimity of sexual union in marriage

St. Francis on scholarship for his *fratres minores* because, indeed, there lurks in it a danger of pride? Or should we see in reason something evil because of the danger of rationalism?

No! Great and terrible as is the danger of impurity, true as it is that in our nature there lurks the tendency to respond to the appeal of the isolation of sex, this in no way alters the fact that the valid, real meaning of this sphere is to be a field of fulfillment for spousal love and that the original, valid aspect of the marital act is its function as a mutual self-donation in the sacred bond of marriage, the constitution of an irrevocable union, and that it is thus as such not something evil, but on the contrary, something great, noble, and pure.

Thus, instead of saying that the sinful satisfaction of sexual desire becomes legitimate through marriage, we should say that the sexual act, because it is destined to be the consummation of this sublime union and fulfillment of spousal love, becomes sinful when desecrated by isolation.

This does not contradict St. Paul when he mentions marriage also as a remedy for concupiscence.[27] Given the fact that in many persons the isolated sexual desire threatens to lead them to sin — that is, to a desecration of the bodily union according to the words of the same St. Paul: "Or do you not know that he who cleaves to a harlot becomes one body with her?"[28] — marriage, in which the bodily union serves the *becoming one flesh*, is also a remedy for concupiscence. But the *ut avertatur peccatum* (that sin may be averted) is not a substitute

[27] 1 Cor. 7:2.
[28] 1 Cor. 6:16.

for spousal love. It means only that the one who is tormented by temptations of an isolated sexual desire should rather marry than remain unwed. But it does not mean that it would be superfluous for him to find a person whom he loves, because it belongs to this *remedy* that, to the greatest extent possible, the marital act becomes the expression of spousal love and the constitution of a lasting, irrevocable bond.

A neutral approach is as bad as a puritanical attitude

Some people argue that sex is not an evil impulse, but rather a natural, good instinct, and that, if there is no special vocation to virginity, it should find its appeasement in the service of procreation, although exclusively, of course, within the framework of marriage. They oppose the negative, puritanical aspects and stress the fact that the sexual instinct is something which belongs to our human nature. An example of this approach is to be found in a recent article on marriage in *France Today* by André Maurois. I quote: "They want marriage to be a happy mixture of comradeship, sexuality, and affection." Such a view fails completely to see that the sexual sphere only reveals its true quality when it is formed by spousal love, serving the constitution of an irrevocable, God-sanctioned union. True marriage is not a mixture of affection or comradeship with a sexuality which remains an autonomous instinct. Rather, the marital act is an organic expression of spousal love.

Whether one sees the sexual desire in a positive or in a negative light is not the decisive point. Rather, the point is that one must see that this instinct is precisely not destined to remain an instinct as other instincts but is destined to become an expression of spousal love, and an ultimate self-donation serving the constitution of the union of both spouses.

Even if one sees sexuality merely as something parallel to the spiritual union — a kind of analogy in the bodily sphere — one still remains blind to the mystery, to the high value of the *mysterium unionis* and to the *mysterium iniquitatis* in its abuse.

This character of mystery is especially overlooked today, and many proclaim it to be a great step forward that instead of a puritanical hush-hush, one now speaks in an open and neutral manner of this sphere. In reality, this is no progress at all. Little as the prim attitude does justice to this sphere, the neutral attitude does it still less justice.

The error of Victorian prudery

Yet it is right to reject Victorian prudery which everywhere scents something impure, which sees sex as something impure in itself, and which favors a shame such as we have for ugly things. For, as I pointed out in my book *In Defense of Purity*, shame and shyness are very different feelings.

Shame wants to hide ugly things, whether they are physical or psychical. We feel shame when others speak of our cowardice or our weakness.

But shyness, which is often confused with shame, reveals our reluctance to exhibit beautiful and noble things if they are intimate. We do not want public scrutiny when we are deeply moved, as when those tears come to our eyes which are the expression of being touched by something beautiful and great. We do not want witnesses when we kiss our spouse. This shyness, referring to things which we hide not because we believe them to be ugly but because they are intimate and their specific value calls for secrecy, is absolutely the right response to the sphere of sex. When it fades away, it is a univocal symptom of becoming blind to the specific nature of sex.

To oppose Victorian prudery by the neutralization of sex, to tear down the walls of this mysterious garden and to see in it *progress*, is a fundamental error.

Here, as so often happens, one opposes a negative attitude not by its real positive counterpart, but by another negative attitude. (Similarly, one erroneously opposes sentimentality, for instance, with an anti-affective neutrality, not seeing that the real antithesis to sentimentality is the true, glorious affectivity, a great ardent love.) And the true antithesis to rationalism is not a ban on reason, the cult of the irrational, but the right use of reason.

So, we must understand that the true antithesis to Victorian prudery is a reverent attitude toward sex, seeing in it something great, deep, and mysterious, whose existence one should not try to deny, but which by its very nature is intimate, and has the character of a secret.

A further fault in Victorian prudery is a behaving as if the realm of sex did not exist. This is obviously something different from dealing with a sphere at a reverent distance, due to its character of a mystery. The prude, who tries to behave as if sex did not exist, has something false and insincere about him; he smacks of a repressed sexuality.

The sublimity of sexual union in marriage

The true antithesis to this prudery is the full admission of the value of this sphere, not hesitating to mention it when it is necessary, but always speaking in a reverent way which does full justice to its character as an intimate mystery and which never neutralizes it.

Chapter Five

⊰⊱

The beauty of children
as the fruit of love

※

The lack of neutrality, the depth and existential impact of the bodily union also discloses itself if one realizes that to this deepest expression of love is confided the coming into existence of a new human being.

In this respect we must also pierce through to the human universe to free ourselves from the before-mentioned superstition that the real, authentic aspect of the world is offered to us exclusively in natural science. As long as we do not understand what a human person is and do not see the abyss separating man from a mere animal, as long as the mystery of personhood is not grasped, then the greatness of the birth of a human being, his coming into existence, cannot be understood. As long as conception and birth are seen exclusively as mere physiological processes, we cannot understand the impact and seriousness of the making of a new human being.

But if we have succeeded in liberating ourselves from this blindness to the authentic reality of the human universe, we cannot but grasp the beauty of the fact that it is to this love union that the engendering of a new human being has been entrusted. As soon as we grasp the beauty of this fact, as soon as we come to understand that the same event which is mutual self-donation and fulfillment of the love-union is the source of a new human being, the reverence and respect with which we should approach this sphere become all the more evident.

To this sublime love union God has confided the coming into being of a new man, a cooperation with his divine creativity. And it must be emphasized that this stress on the meaning and value of marriage as love union does not minimize but rather enhances the link between marriage and procreation.

༻

Instrumental finality vs. superabundance

This will become clearer when we have compared instrumental finality and that finality which we call superabundant finality. In instrumental finality, the being which is considered a means is completely dependent upon the end for its meaning and value.

For example, in the case of a knife, the end — cutting — determines its entire nature; its meaning is identical with serving this end, and its value depends upon its function as a means. Its only *raison d'être* is to be a means for cutting. This is a typical instrumental finality.

In superabundant finality, however, the means has a meaning and value independent of the end to which it leads. Knowledge provides a good example of superabundant finality. We cannot deny that one end of knowledge is to enable man to act. From the most primitive activities to the most complicated ones, our entire practical life presupposes knowledge.

Moreover, a still more sublime end of knowledge is to enable us to attain the moral perfection and sanctification which

74

The beauty of children as the fruit of love

is the presupposition for our eternal welfare. And yet, although these can rightly be called the ends to which knowledge is destined, knowledge, of itself, has undoubtedly also a meaning and value of its own; and the relation to the ends it serves has the character of superabundance. This is a typical case of superabundant finality in which the end is not the exclusive *raison d'être* of something.

This kind of finality differs patently from the instrumental finality which is in question when we call a surgical instrument a means for operating, money a *means* for procuring ourselves a good, or teeth a *means* for the chewing of food.

In other words, in instrumental finality, the end is the exclusive *raison d'être* of the means; in superabundant finality, the means (i.e., the good serving the end) has also a *raison d'être* in itself.

Conjugal union is not merely a means to procreation

We saw before that marriage has intrinsic meaning and value as the deepest and closest love union. We saw that the conjugal act has meaning as a unique fulfillment of this love in mutual self-donation and in its character of constituting a matchless union.

But to that high good, which has a meaning and value in itself, has also been entrusted procreation. The same act, which in its meaning is the constitution of the union, has been superabundantly made the source of procreation, so that we must speak of procreation as the end of marriage, but not in the sense of mere instrumental finality.

Man, Woman, and the Meaning of Love

Whereas we may legitimately consider the sexual instinct in animals to be merely a means to achieve continuation of the species (the *end,* in the sense of an instrumental finality), this patently impossible with respect to the love between man and woman or to their union in marriage.

Occasionally, some persons have conceded that in the subjective approach the spouses need not look at marriage and the conjugal union as a mere means in the instrumental sense; but these same persons have gone on to claim that, objectively, the relation between both has the character of an instrumental finality.

They have asserted that God has implanted in their hearts the love between man and woman and the desire for a conjugal union as a mere means for procreation. But in saying so, they have not understood the real character of the link existing between marriage and procreation.

Mere instincts and urges
can be instrumental means

We touch here on a general and dangerous tendency to overlook the very nature of the person and to assume that the kind of instrumentality which is to be found in the biological realm can be extended to the spiritual realm of man.

As long as instincts or urges are in question, their inner logic and *ratio* goes, so to speak, over the head of the person. It is true that neither man's intelligence nor his free will establishes the meaningful direction of an instinct such as thirst or the desire to sleep.

The beauty of children as the fruit of love

God has given to these instincts and urges their meaning-fulness without involving man's intelligence; this finality is similar to the one found in merely unconscious physiological processes. Insofar as the experienced urge or instinct of thirst, for instance, is at stake, we thus rightly say that its *raison d'être* is to procure for the body the necessary liquid and that God has installed it as a means to that end.

Spiritual acts have value in themselves

But when it comes to spiritual acts of the person (such as willing, loving, or experiencing contrition), we can no longer assume that in the eyes of God they have no meaning in themselves but are only means linked to an end by a similar kind of finality as the instincts or urges. We must not forget that God takes man as a person so seriously that He has addressed Himself directly to man, and that man's free response determines whether or not he will attain his eternal destiny.

The spiritual attitudes of man have a meaning and a *ratio* in themselves, and they can never be treated as having their real significance independently of the person; they involve a person's intelligence, his freedom, and his capacity to respond meaningfully, and not an impersonal, automatic finality going over the person's head. Consequently, it is impossible to see them as attitudes which have their real significance beyond and independently of the person's conscious experience. Man is not a puppet for God but a personal being to whom God addresses Himself and from whom He expects a meaningful response.

Man, Woman, and the Meaning of Love

Devaluation and degradation of the spiritual human attitudes are incompatible with the character of man as a person, his character of *imago Dei*; it ignores the very fact that God has revealed Himself to man and also the way in which man's redemption took place.

Someone might object to this by claiming that God often uses an evil attitude as a means for something good in the life of the individual and especially in the history of mankind. May not an attitude which is evil in itself become a means leading to something good? Yes, indeed, but the *felix culpa* does not remove from the fault its morally negative character and does not entitle us to look at a moral decision as something which acquires its real meaning only in its possible function as *felix culpa*, instead of seeing its primary meaning in its moral value or disvalue.

The kind of finality which we have in mind when we say that God's Providence makes out of evil something leading to a good, differs obviously also in a radical way from the instrumental finality with which we are confronted in the biological sphere. Finality in the former case is not rooted in the nature of something, but comes about through a free intervention of God's Providence in which he uses something in a direction which may even be opposed to its nature and meaning. It would obviously make no sense to say that the end of moral evil is to lead to something good. That would be to claim that the very nature of a moral fault makes it a means for bringing about a good.

The *culpa* is as such *infelix*; the fact that it may become *felix* is owing to an intervention of God, which never entitles us to say that this is the objective, valid meaning of moral guilt in God's eyes. Thus we see that the merciful intervention of God, making a good grow out of evil, in no way dissolves the meaning of a spiritual human attitude, in no way reduces the role of man to that of a puppet.

Procreation is the superabundant end of marriage

Coming back to our topic, we must state that it is incompatible with the very nature of the person to consider the deepest human spiritual experiences as mere subjective aspects of something which, in God's eyes, is a means for an extrinsic end.

It would be dealing with man in a merely biological light if we assumed that love between man and woman, the highest earthly good, is a mere means for the conservation of the species, that its objective *raison d'être* is exclusively to instigate a union which serves procreation.

The God-given, essential link between love of man and woman and its fulfillment in the marital union on the one hand, and the creation of a new person on the other hand, has precisely the character of superabundance, which is a much deeper connection than the one of merely instrumental finality.

But let it be stated again emphatically: stress on the meaning and value of marriage as the most intimate indissoluble union of love does not contradict the doctrine that procreation is the primary end of marriage. The distinction between *meaning* and *end* as well as stress on the fact that marriage has a value of its own besides the sublime value it has as the source of procreation, in no way diminishes the importance of the link between marriage and procreation, but rather enhances it and places it in the right perspective. To stress that the finality in question has the character of superabundance in no way implies a denial of procreation as the primary end of marriage.

The irreverence of artificial contraception

We have now reached the point at which we are able to see the abyss which separates the use of natural family planning from artificial contraception.

The sinfulness of artificial contraception is rooted in the fact that one arrogates to oneself the right to separate the actualized love union in marriage from a possible procreation, to sever this wonderful, deeply mysterious connection, instituted by God, and to approach this mystery in an irreverent attitude. We are here confronted with the basic sin of irreverence toward God, the denial of our creaturehood, the acting as if we were our own lords. It is a basic denial of the *religio,* of our being bound to God; it is a disrespect for the mysteries of God's creation which increases in its sinfulness the higher the rank of the mystery in question.

It is the same sinfulness which lies in suicide or euthanasia, in both of which we act as if we were masters of life. It is the same irreverence which ignores the indissolubility of marriage and in which marriages are contracted and ended as one would change gloves.

Every active intervention on the part of the spouses, which eliminates the possibility of conception through the conjugal act, is incompatible with the holy mystery of the superabundant relation in the incredible gift offered by God.

And this irreverence also affects the purity of the conjugal act because the union can be the real fulfillment of love only when it is approached with reverence and when it is embedded in the *religio*, the consciousness of our basic bond to God.

To the sublime link between marriage and procreation the words of Christ also apply: "What God has joined together, let no man put asunder."[29]

How contraception differs from natural family planning

This irreverence is, however, exclusively connected with the active intervention which severs the conjugal act from its possible link with procreation.

The conjugal act does not in any way lose its full meaning and value if one knows that a conception is out of the question, as when age, an inevitable operation for the sake of health, or pregnancy exclude it. The knowledge that a conception is not in question does not in any way taint the conjugal act with irreverence. This act in such a marriage, if it is the expression of a deep love anchored in Christ, will rank even higher in its quality and its purity than that in a marriage in which the love is less deep and not formed by Christ even though it leads to a conception.

Yet even when, for good and valid reasons (such as the endangering of life or grave economic misery), conception should

[29] Mark 10:9.

as far as possible be avoided, the marital act, whose meaning and value is the actualization of an ultimate union, in no way loses its *raison d'être*. The intention to avoid conception does not imply irreverence as long as one does not actively interfere in order to frustrate the link existing between the conjugal act and a possible conception.

Nor is the use of natural family planning in order to avoid conception in any way irreverent, because the very fact of the possibility of natural family planning, that is to say, the fact that conception is limited to a short period, includes also a God-given institution. This also has a meaning, and it is definitely reverent to accept the opportunity which God offers to those spouses for whom the avoidance of conception is imperative.

That conception is restricted to a short time also implies a word of God. It not only confirms that the bodily union of the spouses has a meaning and value in itself apart from procreation but it also leaves open the possibility of avoiding conception if this is imperative for serious reasons. To make use of natural family planning is not to imply the slightest irreverence or rebellion against God's institution and the wonderful link between the love union and procreation; it is in no way a subterfuge, as some Catholics tend to believe. On the contrary, it is a grateful acceptance of the possibility granted by God to avoid conception, if this is imperative, without frustrating the expression and fulfillment of spousal love in the bodily union.

As soon as we see the abyss which separates the use of natural family planning from artificial contraception, we have answered the rhetorical question: "Why should artificial contraception be a sin if the use of natural family planning is allowed?" And as soon as we see clearly the sinfulness of artificial contraception, we can and must clearly repudiate the suggestion that this is the proper means to avert the threat of overpopulation. No evil in the world, great as it may be, entitles us to use a means for avoiding it which is sinful. To commit a sin in order to avoid an evil would involve adhering to the ignominious principle, "the end justifies the means."

Marriage and the problem of overpopulation

Still, there is little doubt that it is imperative to do something about the threat of overpopulation.

We can rightly hope that science will soon provide us with a means for detecting the days of fecundity in such a strict manner that the use of natural family planning will become a reliable way of avoiding conception. Pope Pius XII said that he prayed ardently that such a means might be found.[30] Since then, important progress is being made in this direction.

However, in circumstances as they exist today, the whole discussion of the problem reveals a distressing moral blindness. It is astonishing that whereas so many voices are raised to demand that the sin of artificial contraception be encouraged by public authority as the best solution to this problem, no one (to the best of my knowledge) has called for an immediate prohibition of the sin of artificial insemination.

[30] *The Pope Speaks,* 45.

Man, Woman, and the Meaning of Love

Artificial insemination is the most vicious separation of procreation from the love union of man and woman; it presupposes the grave sin of masturbation; it implies the meanest, most horrible desecration by placing the begetting of man lower than the natural begetting of a beast, that is, on the level of an injection. It combines the utmost irreverence with the meanest abuse and degradation.

It may be objected that even if we grant the immorality and baseness of artificial insemination, would it not be a totalitarian interference in the life of the individual if it were prohibited by the state?

⚭

The limits of governmental authority

This is a problem of another order: the legitimate interference of the state in private life. The threat of overpopulation does indeed raise this problem also.

In an epoch in which totalitarianism is developed to a full extent in many countries and in which certain totalitarian trends can be witnessed even in democratic countries, we must be particularly watchful of the borderline between the things which by their nature are within the competence of the state and those which belong to the private realm of the individual. There are things which by their very nature should be submitted to state law and eventually enforced, such as those which endanger the individual's life or affect the common good.

But there are many other human and even high moral problems which by their very nature are not within the realm of competence of the state and either should not or cannot be enforced upon the individual.

Thus, a crime must be punished because, apart from the immorality which it implies, it also affects the common good. But it would be patently wrong for the state to try to impose charity or humility by law, or to enforce through police action a certain time of meditation and contemplation in the daily lives of individuals. Equally, the questions of what profession one may choose or whom he may want to marry belong to the sacrosanct realm of the individual which is subject only to God and, insofar as moral commandments are in question, to the Church.

Yet clear as this borderline is in principle, extraordinary circumstances may blur it to a certain extent. The question of how many children a couple has is, as such, patently not within the realm of competence of the state. The state has not the right to forbid a marriage in which children cannot be expected, nor to enforce a marriage in which children can be expected, nor to set a quota for children.

But in such an extraordinary case as the threat of overpopulation which might radically change the entire basis of human existence, the question of interference by the state in order to protect the most elementary common good becomes a serious problem.

Thus, it is clear that the prohibition of something which is a sin and an abominable abuse (such as artificial insemination) has in no way a totalitarian character when it is imperative for the common good. But it is incomprehensible, although perhaps symptomatic, that so many have raised their voices in favor of something immoral — government-encouraged artificial contraception — instead of against something immoral and in every respect base and inhuman: artificial insemination.

⁓

Overpopulation in light of
the meaning of marriage

We should approach the problem imposed on mankind by the threat of overpopulation in full awareness of the mystery of marriage as the ultimate union of spousal love and of the mystery that to this love union, the coming into existence of a new human being has been entrusted.

It is only against this background that we can clearly grasp the precise nature of the sin of artificial contraception and thereby come to see clearly that in looking for means to avert the threat of overpopulation we must radically reject artificial contraception as the solution and must, instead, strive to find a way which would make the use of natural family planning a reliable method of avoiding conception.

The threat of overpopulation throws the meaning of marriage into relief in a specific way. In a situation in which many children, instead of being a blessing, may become a grave injury to the common good of humanity, obviously neither marriage nor the conjugal act lose their justification, meaning, and value. While, until now, a nation has always considered an increase of population as a great common good — a consideration which once assumed a unique character and a higher significance in the elect people of Israel — today the increase of population threatens to become a calamity.

The beauty of children as the fruit of love

Could anyone claim that this new situation also affects the vocation of marriage, that fewer people should get married, or that a man and a woman, loving each other with spousal love, should renounce the union of marriage for the sake of avoiding the increase of population?

Or could one even claim that the bodily union loses, by that, its justification, and that one should encourage married people to live in abstinence, though they feel not the slightest vocation for a virginal marriage? Or may one argue that man's intervention by artificial contraception is warranted by circumstances even though it is a sin? Certainly the answers to all these questions must be in the negative.

If God, through circumstances, imposes the duty of avoiding conception, he does not thereby ostracize the greatest human good on earth, the deepest source of happiness in life — spousal love, and its fulfillment in the sacred union of marriage in which "two shall be one flesh."[31]

[31] Gen. 2:24.

Chapter Six

☘

The moral implications of sexuality

Until now we have only analyzed the nature and purpose of sex without considering its moral aspect. We saw that the humdrum and neutralized view of sex, which sees in it a mere instinct, is wrong (apart from all moral considerations) because it is equivalent to a complete blindness to the true nature of sex. We also saw that this view of sex keeps it from bestowing a great and deep happiness on us as the ultimate expression of love in marriage.

Yet in understanding the mystery of sex, we cannot fail to see the moral relevance in the abuse of this sphere. It is not only that we deprive ourselves, by this abuse, of a deep happiness; in doing so we also act immorally. Desecration is one of the classical sources of moral disvalues. No one doubts that a person who would use the devotion and friendship of another person only to satisfy his egoistic interest, who would make it a mere means for attaining certain profits, in a word, who would abuse devotion and friendship would do something morally base and mean. The very reason for this moral disvalue is precisely the desecration involved in using something noble (which calls for reverence and gratitude) as a mere means for one's own egoistic interests. So it is morally base and mean to give the wrong response to the very nature and value of the sphere of sex, to make something which is destined to be the expression of the deepest human love-communion a mere means for the satisfaction of our instincts.

Some people grant that it is morally wrong to abuse another person for our egoistic interests (e.g., to force someone to overwork himself because we want to make more money). But, with regard to sexual intercourse, they ask how — if both partners desire it — there can be any question of abusing the other, of not respecting his freedom? Why should this be morally wrong?

Apart from the fact that all morality cannot be restricted to not injuring another person, it is wrong to believe that we only injure another person when we impose something on him against his will. The fact that another person likes it does not yet determine whether it is really in his best interest, a real objective good for him. If I know that someone is in danger of becoming an alcoholic and I invite him to drink with me, he may like it very much; but undoubtedly I wrong him in doing so. If someone wants to experience the effect of heroin for the sake of curiosity and I procure him this opportunity, I wrong him, though he may enjoy it. This is certainly a very different case than the one of sexual desire, but it shows that the question whether someone likes it is in no way decisive.

In the misuse of sex, it is certainly not the person's health which is hurt, as in the case of the alcoholic or the addict. But here it is something even more precious which I hurt in him: his dignity as a person. In inducing him to abuse the bodily union or even only yielding to his desire for such an abuse, I degrade his dignity as a person — first, because he becomes a means for my pleasure; and second, because I accept the fact that he throws himself away, that he betrays his secret, that he accomplishes a false self-donation, and that he stains himself by a desecration.

Apart from this immoral attitude toward the other, this disrespect and lack of charity against him, the very throwing away of *oneself* is something immoral. We also have moral obligations toward ourselves.

If someone marries another person only for financial reasons, he commits a base action. He uses so great a good as marriage, which includes the gift of our heart and body to another person, as a means to make money. He sells himself, as it were, by that.

Even if the other person is not deceived and even if he knows about the base motive, nonetheless this selling of oneself, of one's heart and body, is immoral and degrading. Similarly the desecration of the mysterious bodily union of two persons is immoral and base. I wrong myself and the other person in cheating myself and him of the great gift which spousal love can bestow.

Moral good and evil

The *face of the universe* is falsified as soon as one ostracizes the fundamental category of morally good and evil, which is the axis of the spiritual universe and human life and which plays the same role for them as the sun does for the material world surrounding us. We spoke at length about the fundamental error of restricting reality to the laboratory aspect. Now the worst part of this distorted view of the universe is the artificial stripping of the world of its moral substance, the looking at man and his life in a way which neutralizes them from a moral point of view.

As soon as a person artificially denies the tremendous reality of moral good and evil, he blinds himself to the true nature of the human universe. With this denial, all depth, all tension, all spiritual reality are eliminated. This extends even to literature. If we eliminate artificially from *Othello* the categories of good and evil, the moral horror of Iago, the tragic guilt of Othello, the purity and innocence of Desdemona, then instead of this overwhelming tragedy you have something without depth, without tension, without poetry. In seeing each person as the product of complexes and so on, one is transported, as it were, into the domain of psychoanalysis, which certainly (even for those who believe in this type of modern magician) is not a realm of artistic beauty.

Moral good and evil are such elementary realities that even when a philosopher or psychologist tries to deny them, he is faced with them again as soon as he quits his desk and comes again into an existential contact with reality.

The attempt to separate reality from its moral significance is mostly the result of a misconception of morality. One may see morality in the light of a merely positive law; one may believe that it is more or less arbitrarily superimposed, equivalent even to the innumerable taboos with which things have been labeled in human history. It may be that some moralists themselves are guilty of this misconception in handling morality in this way. But, in fact, moral values or disvalues are rooted in the innermost core of things. They are so much the opposite of a superimposition that we blind ourselves from the beginning to the true nature of something if we try to look at it as if it were in a universe where there is no good and evil.

True morality reflects the beauty of sexuality

This applies in a special way to the sphere of sex. If people simply assert that sexual pleasure is sinful and that it is forbidden by the moral law, without seeing the high positive value that sex has in its true and valid function, without recognizing the mystery of sex, this moral judgment may evoke the impression of a superimposed prohibition. Some people try to give a psychological explanation for the alleged taboo on extramarital intercourse, believing that in liberating this sphere from the taboo, in denying any moral significance to it, they have made life healthier and happier. These people believe that in neutralizing sex from the moral point of view, they finally approach it in a positive way.

In reality, the moral significance of this sphere is indissolubly linked with its true nature, with its true value, with the mystery it embodies. And in trying to draw sex out of the moral universe, they do not open the way for a healthy approach to sex, do not make life happier, but rather close the door on the true approach to sex. They make man blind to its true value; they bar the stream of deep happiness which it is destined to bestow on human life in marriage. Instead of freeing man, they imprison him in hopeless boredom.

Man, Woman, and the Meaning of Love

It is not difficult to see the abyss which yawns between the concept of sexual intercourse as the satisfaction of a mere bodily instinct like hunger and thirst, and the concept of bodily union as the highest, most mysterious fulfillment of spousal love in the bond of marriage. It is not difficult to see in which concept sex bears a higher value.

But this cannot be grasped without also seeing that the abuse of something so deep and mysterious is a grave moral fault. We saw the moral disvalue of the desecration of that which is destined to be the deep and mysterious fulfillment of spousal love. We now must add that it is an enormous degradation of sex — not only drawing it down to a much lower level, but depriving it of all its true value — if one tries to exempt it from the moral sphere, to separate it from its moral significance. This is tantamount to dispossessing sex from its capacity to be a source of real happiness.

How the moral aspect is indissolubly linked to grasping the true nature of sex becomes obvious as soon as we compare two different cases. In the first, an isolated sexual desire or a superficial intoxication which assumes the character of an overwhelming passion brings someone to a fall. He is clearly aware of the moral evil which he is committing. He sees the mystery of the sexual sphere, its depth, its intimacy, and its impact. He succumbs to the aspect which this sphere also can have, a mysterious, diabolical attraction.

In this case, there is the terrible desecration, but at least he still sees the mystery of this sphere because he is aware of the desecration, and because he grasps the moral abyss into which he is falling.

In the second case, the man who on the contrary sees sex as morally neutral and sexual intercourse as a normal satisfaction of a healthy instinct such as eating, misses completely the nature of sex. He is blind to its intimacy, depth, impact, and mystery. He is completely incapable of understanding the role of the bodily union as fulfillment of a deep spousal love; he is cut off from the deep happiness which sex is destined to bestow on man.

Amorality is still worse than immorality. The immoral man can repent his moral failure; he turns back to his depth. But the amoral man has condemned himself to the periphery and finds no way back when he commits something objectively immoral.

The one who falls morally but is aware of his immorality remains still in the orbit of truth. He acknowledges the ultimate importance of the moral question, even if he goes astray in this moment. He still moves in the true spiritual universe and sees the true values. His situation may be tragic. But the one who desecrates the mystery of sex by seeing in it a harmless satisfaction of a bodily instinct, who approaches the world having extinguished the light of morality, moves in a dull, falsified world without depth, without thrill, without grandeur. His world is the magnified office of a psychoanalyst. He is not tragic; rather, he is immersed in hopeless boredom because it is the moral light, the great tension of good and evil, which elevates and widens human life beyond the frontiers of our earthly existence. As Kierkegaard said, "The ethical is the very breath of the eternal."

Chapter Seven

◽

Friendship between man and woman

⚜

In our day, one particularly topical question concerns the divinely willed significance of man and woman toward one another *outside* of the married state. Does the difference of the two sexes have a significance and a meaningful function for other kinds of relationships or is its God-willed purpose limited to marriage: the closest, highest, and most complete of all the fundamentally rooted communions?

This question is quickly answered for those who admit only the sexual sphere as the basic reason why men and women were destined for each other. The sexual sphere is unequivocally associated with marriage; it may, according to the divine intention, be actualized only in marriage. This is so self-evident for every Catholic, yes, for every morally conscious person, that to waste any words on that here would be carrying owls to Athens. So if the intended association of man and woman really existed exclusively in the sexual sphere, we could immediately answer our question: the significance of man and woman for one another begins and ends in marriage.

But anyone who undertakes a profound inquiry into the significance of man and woman for one another within marriage (as I have attempted in my book *In Defense of Purity*), will soon recognize that even here the specific supplementary characteristic is not limited to the sexual sphere. In fact, one can only come to understand the deeper meaning of the sexual sphere as the particular fulfillment of spousal love once one grasps the unique possibility of *spiritual* fulfillment between man and woman and once one sees that sexual completion is only a particular expression of the spiritual enrichment.

A true understanding of the greatness and consecration of marriage — that final, supreme state of mutual love which has been compared to the relationship of Christ to the Church — as well as any profound comprehension of the specific nature of spousal love, leads directly to the insight that an entirely unique spiritual enrichment between persons is the issue here, long before the sexual sphere comes into consideration. This spiritual replenishment is of a nature that is only possible between men and women, but never between man and man or woman and woman. To understand the unique spiritual supplementary quality of man and woman, one must first realize that the difference between them is not merely biological but is rather a profound distinction affecting the basic structure of the personality, and that this difference has its own value. The difference is metaphysical, as the Pythagoreans rightly suspected when they — although with inadmissible exaggeration — made two categories of Being out of masculine and feminine.

Persons are not merely higher animals

With this question we touch on a frequent, though radically mistaken view of man. It attempts to understand man from below, from the animal-like, instead of seeing in him the image of God. Thus, it holds that all those things in man which can be tied to the physiological-biological sphere are the more intrinsic and the more real aspects. It attempts to interpret spiritual acts (such as loving, willing, longing, and enthusiasm) as merely highly developed drives. It attempts to interpret the *meaningful* connections between motivations as *causally determined* associations. It seeks to understand the structure of the human person and its innately given differentiations as pure functions of biological-physiological ends.

In short, it takes those aspects of man which he shares with higher organisms to be the fundamentally real ones, and seeks to understand that which is spiritual in him as being only a refinement of the vital, biological sphere — the latter constituting the deeper, the actual foundation.

Such a conception, which is exemplified in the ridiculous idea that man, a spiritual person who executes meaningful acts, could have developed out of an animal (like a higher species out of a lower one) misunderstands the nature of man totally. This conception does not recognize the *essential* difference between a spiritual person and a mere living creature, a distinction which is so fundamental that the difference between an amoeba and a monkey disappears in comparison. In fact, this difference is even much deeper and more fundamental than the one between material objects and living beings.

For the person who has freed himself from this basically mistaken tendency, which still haunts modern psychology, it is not difficult to see that the difference between man and woman is not only a biological one, but that it concerns two different original types of the spiritual person that is man. Although we must also guard against the not uncommon exaggeration of this difference, it still remains correct that in man and woman we are confronted with two fundamental types of mankind, with their specific values, with their specific missions, and with their specific supplementary gifts.

Men and women share the same ultimate calling

To begin with, we would like to point out briefly the three directions in which this distinction is being painfully exaggerated, in order then to clarify the magnitude of the positive differences.

The difference between man and woman cannot and does not affect mankind's ultimate calling: to be transformed in Christ, to become holy, to glorify God, and to reach eternal communion with Him. In the confrontation of creature and Creator the difference between man and woman disappears entirely.

In reference to the rebirth in Christ, to the receiving of supernatural life, no difference exists. Also here the Word prevails: *one* baptism, *one* belief, *one* sacrifice. Every eternal soul, whether it belongs to a man or a woman, has the task to actualize and radiate Christ with its *entire* being and not with only a part of itself. It is wrong to claim that two different roads to the final goal exist here for men and women. But this does not eliminate the factor of femininity or masculinity from the specific individual note to be found even in the saints. In fact, it serves to give a particular hue to their universal holiness.

Friendship between man and woman

The same exaggeration of the distinction between the sexes is found in the frequent attempts to interpret the commandments for moral perfection and holiness differently for men than for women. Again and again one hears the totally false statement that, as far as purity is concerned, the commandments are stricter for women than for men, and other arguments of the same brand. The difference between man and woman does not imply a difference in moral standards.

The development of masculinity and femininity

A second, quite different danger of this exaggeration occurs when one makes of *masculinity* or *femininity* a conscious goal to strive for; that is, when one does not see that man and woman both must simply strive for the right and the God-willed, and that the difference between the two sexes, in fact, becomes quite distinct all by itself.

This is just as distressing as when someone constantly emphasizes his own particular individuality and, instead of simply striving for the objectively right, only concentrates on the preservation of his own personality. The specific tone of the feminine and masculine must appear by itself and color the result; it must not occupy the mind during the fulfillment of objective demands unless their subject matter is directly relevant to the person's sex.

Such a reaction is, then, only justified when certain particular questions are concerned, which in themselves already have a particular relationship to the nature of the feminine or the masculine.

Man, Woman, and the Meaning of Love

For instance, for a woman, many things take on an abandoned, unseemly character which are perfectly natural for a man. But even here it is much less artificial, much more precious if the woman instinctively omits the unfitting than if she first has to reflect upon and remember her femininity. The same holds *mutatis mutandis* for the man. Normally, this particular coloring must appear by itself, analogously, for instance, to the national peculiarities. An artist who wants to create *German* art affects us with a sort of embarrassment. If he is a German and wants to create *good* art, the specifically national tone appears by itself. Conscious self-reflection leads to irrelevance and an awkward *feeling like a man* or *feeling like a woman*.

⚭

The phony war between the sexes
This leads us straight to the third type of exaggeration. This *feeling like a man* — or *a woman* — can lead to a special communal feeling among each of the sexes, even to the point of seeing women and men as two opposing interest groups. Many men and women feel that they belong to a faction and then look at everything from this *partisan* viewpoint. We will return later to the basic fallacy of this attitude.

It is particularly nonsensical for this reason: the more someone truly grasps the essential nature of woman as woman and man as man, the more will he also see their specific complementary nature — the meaning of both for each other — which totally excludes this factional solidarity. This exaggeration results in the actual loss of the particular essence of the sexes. Such women become unfeminine and such men become neuters.

This exaggeration finally ends in an overlooking of the specific character of the masculine and the feminine.

There are many spiritual differences between the sexes

On the other hand, however mistaken these exaggerations are, it remains necessary to clearly recognize the God-willed meaning of *femininity* and *masculinity* apart from the sexual sphere, and to understand the specific value contained in these two shapings of the human person.

It would lead too far here to enumerate all the details of the spiritual particularities of the feminine and masculine person. The specific, organic meld of heart and mind, of the affective and intellective centers in woman, the unity of her entire nature, the delicacy and receptivity of her whole being, the precedence of Being as a personality over objective accomplishments — versus man's specific ability to emancipate the mind from all his vitality, the ability for pure objectivity which predestines him for official positions, his specific suitability for efficacy and the accomplishments of objective works, his clarity, strength, and greatness, these differences mark the two sexes in their own peculiar nature.

We only need think of the holy men and women in order to see how this difference creates a distinct and specific aura. The same love for Jesus lives in both, both are exclusively concerned with the *unum necessarium*, both are totally receptive to God, in both is the same purity, the same meekness, the same heroism, the same victorious strength; and yet each represents the highest form of femininity and masculinity.

Man, Woman, and the Meaning of Love

Can one imagine anything more feminine than the Holy Virgin Mary? Would it not be an impossible idea to imagine exactly the same qualities realized in a man? Her holiness, of course, could be actualized in a man, but the particular aura would then necessarily be different. It is part of the structure of man that there be these two fundamental forms.

In the Middle Ages the depth of this difference was totally understood, as evidenced by the interest in the question of whether the angels were also masculine and feminine. The very question already shows — no matter how one might answer it — that this difference does not only exist in man insofar as he is a living being, but it exists also in *quantum homo*, insofar as he is a spiritual person. There is even a special value in these specific forms; the eradication of this difference is by no means desirable.

The figures of our saints clearly demonstrate that this difference in sex not only continues to exist in the saints, but it appears in them in its most ideal form. We have only to consider St. Agnes, St. Scholastica, St. Elizabeth, St. Catherine of Siena, and St. Thérèse of the Child Jesus on the one hand, and then St. Paul, St. Peter, St. Augustine, St. Benedict, St. Ignatius of Loyola, and St. Bernard on the other, to see clearly that they are each bearers of the specific feminine and masculine values.

The mission of men and women to each other
Whoever penetrates deeply into the spiritual nature of the masculine and feminine also sees the specific design of both

for each other. First, man and woman have a purely spiritual mission toward each other and enrich each other in a way which is not possible with the same sex. Second, a woman will never be as deeply understood by a woman as she could be understood by a man; a man will never be as deeply understood by a man as he could be by a woman.

Two most important moments must be kept apart in examining this mutual destiny: first, the specific mission of the man for the woman and the woman for the man, and second, the possibility of a much closer and more ultimate communion based on their supplementary nature.

Their mission toward each other consists, in part, of the necessity to adjust to the contrasting nature of the other sex, and in the curtailment of certain inimical tendencies inherent in the nature of each of the sexes when they entirely lack the other's influence.

This mission toward each other is, however, not only limited to a negative role, that is, to the compensation of a danger. The spiritual contact of man and woman also has a positive mission, namely, a unique stimulation and mutual spiritual fecundation. Particular virtues in both are awakened which otherwise remain undeveloped. The chivalrous attitude awakens in the man a stronger self-control, a more humble attitude, a greater delicacy and purity, a certain melting and enlivening of his nature. With the woman, on the other hand, a widening of her intellect takes place, a broader and more principle-tied foundation for her sense of values, a noble reserve on one hand and a specific warmth and devotion on the other, appears.

Man, Woman, and the Meaning of Love

Ⅎ

Deep, mutual understanding between men and women

This specific mutual enrichment is closely tied to that second aspect of which we spoke above. The fact that the two natures are ordered toward each other enables a mutual understanding of the deepest kind. A man will accomplish more in the spiritual transformation of a woman, as will a woman with a man. It is no accident that the idea of spiritual guidance is at its purest when the guided person is *female*. This arises from the fact that man and woman can understand each other best, as we saw above.

The supplementary nature of man and woman places them, from the beginning, more in a face-to-face position than side-by-side. It forms the specific foundation for all *I-thou* relationships, for the ultimate interpenetration of two persons, for spiritual union.[32] It is precisely the general dissimilarity in the nature of both which enables this deeper penetration into the soul of the other, a stronger seeing-from-the-inside, an ultimate openness toward the other, a real complementary relationship.

The two types of being are coordinated to each other and, as such, they have been given the specific ability to understand each other. This fact not only constitutes the spiritual foundation for marriage but also, as we will see, the possibility for deeper, closer, more radiant communions of a purely spiritual nature than are ever possible within one sex.

Now that we have begun to recognize the spiritual difference in the nature of man and woman, as well as their specific

[32] See my book *Metaphysik der Gemeinschaft* (Augsburg, 1930).

destiny for each other, our original question of the significance of the two sexes for each other apart from marriage has become twofold. First, apart from marriage, in which individual relationships is this spiritual destiny most effective? What classic types of friendship exist between man and woman? Second, how does this coordination affect large groups which comprise men and women?

*Male/female spiritual relations
are not sublimated desire*

Before we turn to answering these questions, we must still call attention to the following. In Sigmund Freud's theory, everything in the world is led back to sexual motives. Unfortunately, this fundamentally false idea has also entered some Catholic circles in a milder form.

For this conception, the spiritual coordination of man and woman is naturally only the result of their sexual affiliation. Of course, for those who see everything — art, religion, every form of love — as only a sublimation of the sex drive, this spiritual complementarity will also be seen as such, if not as cleverly covert sexuality *per se*.

We cannot go further into the fundamental errors of this theory here. For the time being, we can identify it as a classic case of that false psychology which sees the living being, instead of the spiritual person, as the real substance of man. It is yet another example of that mistaken view *from below* which we mentioned in the beginning. It makes out of the sexual sphere — which, according to its true meaning, is only an

expression of the higher spiritual sphere — the actual foundation of the entire life of the soul.[33] This viewpoint demon-
strates a fundamental misunderstanding of the structure of the
person as well as the wholly sovereign nature of the spiritual
sphere.

But even the person who has seen the principal falseness of
this theory must be careful of the fatal symbolism of detecting a sexual note in everything. If one searches assiduously
enough for a sexual note, one will find it everywhere. But not
because it really is there, but because one puts on spiritual
glasses as it were, which are *sexually tinted*. It is a specific pecu-
liarity of this sphere that one can see everything in its light,
that this way of looking at things is, so to speak, contagious, so
that even when one thinks he has found something completely unconnected, in the next moment it also seems sexually tinted. One has to be on one's guard against this scenting
out of sexuality behind everything — in the relationship of
mother and son, father and daughter, brother and sister, etc.,
because this attitude creates a particular foundation for errors.
One sees *something* in everything, though there is actually
nothing there. And so we must not only totally reject the as-
sertion that every spiritual relationship between man and
woman is repressed sexuality, but also the frequently heard
statement that a purely spiritual friendship or love between
the two sexes cannot exist, that there is always at least some
element of sexuality in it, and that this element cannot be altogether excluded.

[33] See my book *In Defense of Purity*.

❧

Sexual temptation calls for vigilance, not separation

On the other hand, we must not forget that as mistaken as it is to attempt to develop the spiritual coordination of both sexes out of their sexual relationship or even to consider their spiritual relationship as being basically something sexual, yet fallen man is constantly exposed to the danger of a sexual element illegitimately creeping into this relationship. In fallen man, the lower sphere has so emancipated itself from the higher one that it not only actualizes itself in harmony with the higher, spiritual sphere, and particularly in unison with the will, but it also appears in isolated form. Therefore, a leap into the sexual sphere, even an illegitimate one, can always occur in every relationship between the two sexes. The words apply here, too: "Be sober, be vigilant; because your adversary the devil, as a roaring lion, walketh about, seeking whom he may devour."[34] But this danger, while it must exhort us to wakefulness and caution, cannot become a motive for avoiding all contact with the opposite sex.

It is impossible to escape the dangers of temptation. The mere danger of a temptation should certainly keep us away from worthless and indifferent things, but it may not hold us back from things which are in themselves good and wholesome.

The same thing applies here as in the other temptations. Who is safe from pride when he does something good? Shall he therefore omit the deed? The words of St. Bernard, when he was seized by pride over the power of his own preaching

[34] 1 Pet. 5:8.

during a sermon, apply here: "Satan, I did not begin to preach for thee; for thee I will not cease to do it." This general danger of sudden temptations must therefore keep us in constant wakefulness and in a healthy mistrust of ourselves, but it does not constitute sufficient reason for avoiding a spiritual contact with the other person. We will see later that these temptations impose certain obligations upon the communion between the two sexes.

Spiritual communion among the unmarried

We will now turn to the question of the classic types of friendship between the two sexes. It is said that even if the general danger of temptations is no obstacle to the possible association between the sexes, yet, as soon as an outspoken friendship between man and woman develops, a close personal bond, an explicit *I-thou* relationship, a true, loving interpenetration, a shift into the sexual sphere becomes inevitable. In other words, it is said that a deep friendship, filled with a real love, between man and woman is always simultaneously a sexually tinted one, whether the persons in question admit it to themselves or not. If this were correct, any love communion between man and woman outside of marriage would be doomed — but this is definitely not the case.

Of course, we don't want to deceive ourselves. When an ultimate spiritual *I-thou* relationship exists between man and woman, there also exists a natural tendency for this love to lead to the sexual sphere, as is the case in marriage. But there are special factors which uproot this tendency and which preserve the purely spiritual character of this relationship without taking anything away from its depth and ardor.

Of course, this dangerous tendency exists only for those friendships which represent an ultimate *I-thou* relationship and which thereby go vastly beyond any friendship in the ordinary sense. The typical friendship — which consists of a distinct standing beside each other hand in hand, a joint gazing at objective values — is a relationship in which the mutual love is not *thematic*, in which no specific interpenetration of the souls is present and no spiritual unification is intended. Therefore, it does not contain the tendency to slip over to the sexual sphere. The starting point for any possible reference to the sensual sphere is missing in the very quality of this relationship. That such a friendship between man and woman is possible is obvious, and for it to remain free of any sexual admixture is no problem.[35] But in this relationship the special radiance and the centrality of a real *I-thou* relationship, in which a full coordination of man and woman effects its ultimate supplementary meaning, is also missing.

This is our actual problem: which factor can keep an ultimate *I-thou* relationship between both sexes free from every intrinsically normal overlapping into the sexual sphere? When can a relationship be purely spiritual and yet full of ultimate

---

[35] The generally required wakefulness noted above is naturally necessary here, too; for, since man is never safe from sexual temptations, they can suddenly appear here also. But then they come altogether from the outside, i.e., entirely accidentally, since there is no foundation given for them in the relationship itself.

ardor and devotion? Only when it is a communion in Jesus, from Jesus, and for Jesus. Only through being totally anchored in the supernatural can an ultimate *I-thou* relationship remain free of every sexual shadow and yet represent a unique fulfillment of the spiritual mutuality of man and woman. A mutual elevation to the intellectual sphere is not sufficient. We must rise to the spiritual — that is, the supernatural sphere — in order for this holy communion to develop. In this relationship the coordination of man and woman can then unfold in all its value, permitting a spiritual union in Jesus which would never be possible between men or between women.

This presupposes that Jesus is the theme of this relationship, that for each partner the other's salvation is of primary concern, that they each participate in the love of Jesus for the other, that His Sacred Heart is the place where both souls meet and where they, as it were, interpenetrate. This relationship then has a glow and an ardor that cannot be surpassed by any other love-relationship. It is somewhat analogous to spousal love in that respect, but it also has a purity and spirituality which no relationship between persons of the same sex can exceed.[36]

This is not a vague ideal which has never been realized, but an actual possibility which has happened many times in the history of the saints. The most outstanding example is the relationship between St. Francis de Sales and St. Jane Frances de Chantal, whose letters unequivocally demonstrate the depth and ardor, the purity and ultimateness of their relationship.

---

[36] See my book *Metaphysik der Gemeinschaft*, Part I, ch. 3.

But it is immediately apparent to all those who look more deeply that such a fulfillment, such an ultimate mutual understanding, such an interpenetration of souls is, first, only possible in and through Jesus, and second, only possible between man and woman. Let us think of St. Clare and St. Francis of Assisi, of St. Teresa of Avila and St. John of the Cross, and of St. Bernard of Clairvaux, who wrote these words to Countess Ermengard:

> Why can't I bring my spirit just as much before your eyes as I do this paper, thus showing you the feelings of love in my heart which the Lord pours into me, and the zeal for your soul with which He fills me! Truly, you would recognize that no words and no pen can express my feelings. I am with you spiritually, though we are physically separated. It is true, I cannot show you my heart since it is impossible for me to entirely reveal it to you. I depend on you to understand it; you need only to look into your own to find mine therein, and to ascribe to me as much love for you as you feel for me. . . . You will now understand how you have, since my departure, kept me entirely with you, because, for my part, I can truly say that I have not left you when I departed and that I find you everywhere, wherever I go. . . . [M]y heart is at the pinnacle of joy as soon as it receives news of the peace of your heart. I am happy when I know that you are happy, and in your rest I find mine.[37]

---

[37] *Letter 116* in the Benedictine edition.

However, I want to warn emphatically against ranking these spiritual love-relationships — because of their purely spiritual character — above marriage. It is true that they usually stand subjectively higher because they can only exist on the highest level, i.e., in Jesus. But if we think of a marriage on the same level (such as a marriage between two saints), the fact that their union also includes the sexual sphere may not be given as a reason for considering marriage as something less lofty.

The decisive thing is to see that the relationship of man and woman, also outside of marriage, makes possible a purely spiritual communion of singular depth, ardor, and purity, and of particular completion, mutual understanding and enrichment. Through this communion, Jesus (who said, "Wherever two shall meet in my name, there shall I be also"[38]) is glorified. This relationship then embodies a specific *victory* over the world.

⚬

Dangers for male/female relationships in groups

Regarding the role of man and woman's mutual destiny in large communities, it is important to counteract two dangers. The first is the already mentioned general danger of an encroachment into the sexual sphere. The second consists of a blunting that may take place through the association of men and women. These two dangers come strikingly to the fore in high school and college education. This particularly affects

[38] Matt. 18:20.

the woman. It reduces her femininity, thereby annulling the beneficial effect of the two sexes on each other as well as destroying the characteristic individual value of the feminine.

In order to compensate for the second danger it is necessary that the good which unifies the group be either of such a high nature that it requires an elevation of the hearts of all its members — as in the case of religious communities or secular communities in which a certain ideal holds all together — or the good must possess a colorful festivity, as in social affairs in former times. Although the two situations are very dissimilar, they yet possess such a constitutive force that both sexes retain their specific nature and value. Therefore, they have a stimulating, beneficial, and complementary effect on the group atmosphere and on each other.

But if the groups here in question are founded on a strictly pragmatic basis — for instance, if they are centered on economic interests or are based on a mere feeling of comradeship — then the situation is inimical to the nature of woman as woman, and the possibility of influencing and rounding out the atmosphere through her participation is eliminated.

The mission of the sexes for each other can therefore not always simply take effect in every group. It demands certain prerequisites. If these do not exist, and a certain conviviality reigns in the situation, it is better if women are not present.

Chivalry is still necessary

That leads us to another important element which simultaneously contains the compensation of the sexual danger.

Man, Woman, and the Meaning of Love

The association between man and woman must always retain a chivalrous character on the man's side. All rough and ready comradeship is simply unbearable between the two sexes.

When men and women are together, an atmosphere of self-control must reign, i.e., the opposite of *letting oneself go*. That is automatically the case with all groups whose common good is the bearer of high values — above all, in religious communities — because then the height of the field of values leads each person into his depth, unifies him, and produces the opposite of all *letting go* by itself. With social affairs, it is necessary to safeguard the maintaining of a chivalrous attitude, of a noble reticence, and also to avoid all *letting oneself go*, all convivial obtruding.

Today's dances and today's fashions, all the totally traditionless living habits of freely associating youth, prove sufficiently how important these demands are. In all those situations where the common ideal consists of *letting oneself go* — where one feels only then *at home* when one *lets go*, it is better if the sexes remain separated. Otherwise their association is destructive and dangerous. Then this *letting oneself go* is much worse than when it takes place in the company of the same sex. In other words, wherever one consciously supersedes the specific mission of the two sexes for each other, or objectively excludes it, the association of the two sexes is destructive and wrong, just as, analogously, it is still better that, if I want to let myself go, I do this in a bar instead of in a church.

On the other hand, this situation also sheds light on the particular mission inherent in the association of the two sexes in a group. Simply through bringing women into a social affair, everyone is forced to avoid all *letting go* and to go to one's depth.

These thoughts show how great the significance of man and woman is for many types of communities other than marriage, what high values can spring from the spiritual contact of man and woman, how necessary and wholesome their mutual influence is, and how incomplete a merely male or female race would be, apart from the biological impossibility.

But primarily, it becomes apparent from the preceding how ridiculous it is to reinterpret the self-evident common task in this world, in which both are called to collaborate, into a rivalry between the sexes against each other, as if the world were to be looked at from a male and female viewpoint. The complementary role of man and woman is not limited to marriage — rather it enables a more complete communion among all mankind. The word of God at the creation of Eve has general application: "It is not good for man to be alone; let us make him a helper like unto himself."[39]

[39] Gen. 2:18.

Dietrich von Hildebrand

(1889-1977)

❧

Hitler feared him and the late Pope Pius XII called him "the twentieth-century Doctor of the Church." For more than six decades, Dietrich von Hildebrand — philosopher, spiritual writer, and anti-Nazi crusader — led philosophical, religious, and political groups, lectured throughout Europe and the Americas, and published more than thirty books and many more articles. His influence was widespread and endures to this day.

Although von Hildebrand was a deep and original thinker on subjects ranging across the spectrum of human interests, nonetheless, in his lectures and his writings, he instinctively avoided extravagant speculations and convoluted theories. Instead, he sought to illuminate the nature and significance of seemingly "everyday" elements of human existence that are easily misunderstood and too frequently taken for granted.

Therefore, much of von Hildebrand's philosophy concerns the human person, the person's interior ethical and affective life, and the relations that should exist between the person and the world in which he finds himself.

Von Hildebrand's background made him uniquely qualified to examine these topics. He was born in beautiful Florence in

Man, Woman, and the Meaning of Love

1889, the son of the renowned German sculptor, Adolf von Hildebrand. At the time, the von Hildebrand home was a center of art and culture, visited by the greatest European artists and musicians of the day. Young Dietrich's early acquaintance with these vibrant, creative people intensified his natural zest for life.

In Florence, von Hildebrand was surrounded by beauty — the overwhelming natural beauty of the Florentine country-side and the rich beauty of the many art treasures that are Florence's Renaissance heritage. Pervading this Florentine atmosphere was Catholicism: in the art, in the architecture, and in the daily life of the people. These years in Florence quickened in the young von Hildebrand a passionate love of truth, of goodness, of beauty, and of Christianity.

As he grew older, he developed a profound love for philosophy, studying under some of the greatest German philosophers of the early twentieth century, including Edmund Husserl, Max Scheler, and Adolf Reinach. Converting to Catholicism in 1914, von Hildebrand taught philosophy for many years at the University of Munich.

However, soon after the end of World War I, Nazism began to threaten von Hildebrand's beloved southern Germany. With his characteristic clearsightedness, von Hildebrand immediately discerned its intrinsic evil. From its earliest days, he vociferously denounced Nazism in his articles and in speeches throughout Germany and the rest of Europe.

Declaring himself unwilling to continue to live in a country ruled by a criminal, von Hildebrand regretfully left his native Germany for Austria, where he continued teaching philosophy (at the University of Vienna) and fought the Nazis with even greater vigor, founding and then publishing for a number of years a prominent anti-Nazi newspaper, *Christliche Ständestaat*.

This angered both Heinrich Himmler and Adolf Hitler, who were determined to silence von Hildebrand and to close his anti-Nazi newspaper. Orders were given to have him assassinated in Austria. However, von Hildebrand evaded the hit-squads and, thanks to his Swiss passport, was finally able to flee the country just as it fell to the Nazis.

It is characteristic of von Hildebrand that even while he was engaged in this dangerous life-and-death struggle against the Nazis, he maintained his deep spiritual life and managed to write during this period his greatest work, the sublime and highly acclaimed spiritual classic, *Transformation in Christ*.

Fleeing from Austria, von Hildebrand was pursued through many countries, ultimately arriving on the shores of America in 1940 by way of France, Spain, Portugal, and Brazil.

Penniless in New York after his heroic struggle against the Nazis, von Hildebrand was hired as a professor at Fordham University where he taught until his retirement. Many of his best works were written during this period and after his retirement. He died in 1977 in New Rochelle, New York.

Dietrich von Hildebrand was remarkable for his keen intellect, his profound originality, his prodigious output, his great personal courage, his deep spirituality, and his intense love of truth, goodness, and beauty. These rare qualities made Dietrich von Hildebrand one of the greatest philosophers and one of the wisest men of the twentieth century.

Sophia Institute Press®

✢

Sophia Institute™ is a nonprofit institution that seeks to restore man's knowledge of eternal truth, including man's knowledge of his own nature, his relation to other persons, and his relation to God. Sophia Institute Press® serves this end in numerous ways: it publishes translations of foreign works to make them accessible for the first time to English-speaking readers; it brings out-of-print books back into print; and it publishes important new books that fulfill the ideals of Sophia Institute™. These books afford readers a rich source of the enduring wisdom of mankind.

Sophia Institute Press® makes these high-quality books available to the general public by using advanced technology and by soliciting donations to subsidize its general publishing costs. Your generosity can help Sophia Institute Press® to provide the public with editions of works containing the enduring wisdom of the ages. Please send your tax-deductible contribution to the address below. We also welcome your questions, comments, and suggestions.

For your free catalog, call:
Toll-free: 1-800-888-9344

Sophia Institute Press® ♦ Box 5284 ♦ Manchester, NH 03108
www.sophiainstitute.com

Sophia Institute™ is a tax-exempt institution as defined by the Internal Revenue Code, Section 501(c)(3). Tax I.D. 22-2548708.